# Microsoft® Office PowerPoint® 2003

## ILLUSTRATED, CourseCard Edition

**BRIEF**

David W. Beskeen

**THOMSON**
**COURSE TECHNOLOGY**™

Australia • Canada • Mexico • Singapore • Spain • United Kingdom • United States

# Microsoft® Office PowerPoint® 2003 — Illustrated Brief, CourseCard Edition

David W. Beskeen

**Managing Editor:**
Marjorie Hunt

**Production Editors:**
Philippa Lehar,
Danielle Slade

**QA Manuscript Reviewer:**
Jeff Schwartz

**Product Managers:**
Christina Kling Garrett,
Jane Hosie-Bounar

**Developmental Editor:**
Rachel Biheller Bunin

**Text Designer:**
Joseph Lee, Black Fish Design

**Associate Product Manager:**
Emilie Perreault

**Editorial Assistant:**
Shana Rosenthal

**Composition House:**
GEX Publishing Services

# The Illustrated Series Vision

Teaching and writing about computer applications can be extremely rewarding and challenging. How do we engage students and keep their interest? How do we teach them skills that they can easily apply on the job? As we set out to write this book, our goals were to develop a textbook that:

- works for a beginning student

- provides varied, flexible, and meaningful exercises and projects to reinforce the skills

- serves as a reference tool

- makes your job as an educator easier, by providing resources above and beyond the textbook to help you teach your course

Our popular, streamlined format is based on advice from instructional designers and customers. This flexible design presents each lesson on a two-page spread, with step-by-step instructions on the left, and screen illustrations on the right. This signature style, coupled with high-caliber content, provides a comprehensive yet manageable introduction to Microsoft Office PowerPoint 2003 — it is a teaching package for the instructor and a learning experience for the student.

## About This Edition

New to this edition is a free, tear-off PowerPoint 2003 CourseCard that provides students with a great way to have PowerPoint skills at their fingertips!

## Acknowledgments

I would like to thank Rachel Biheller Bunin for her tireless efforts and editorial insights, which has made my work better. I would also like to thank Thomson Course Technology for all of their vision and support over the last 10 years; I look forward to many more!

David W. Beskeen
and the Illustrated Team

# Preface

Welcome to *Microsoft® Office PowerPoint® 2003–Illustrated Brief, CourseCard Edition.* Each lesson in this book contains elements pictured to the right.

## How is the book organized?
The book is organized into four units on PowerPoint, covering creating, editing, and formatting presentations.

## What kinds of assignments are included in the book? At what level of difficulty?
The lessons use MediaLoft, a fictional chain of bookstores, as the case study. The assignments on the light purple pages at the end of each unit increase in difficulty. Data Files and case studies, with many international examples, provide a great variety of interesting and relevant business applications. Assignments include:

- **Concepts Reviews** include multiple choice, matching, and screen identification questions.

- **Skills Reviews** provide additional hands-on, step-by-step reinforcement.

- **Independent Challenges** are case projects requiring critical thinking and application of the unit skills. The Independent Challenges increase in difficulty, with the first one in each unit being the easiest (most step-by-step with detailed instructions). Independent Challenges 2 and 3 become increasingly open-ended, requiring more independent problem solving.

- **E-Quest Independent Challenges** are case projects with a Web focus. E-Quests require the use of the World Wide Web to conduct research to complete the project.

- **Advanced Challenge Exercises** set within the Independent Challenges provide *optional* steps for more advanced students.

- **Visual Workshops** are practical, self-graded capstone projects that require independent problem solving.

Each 2-page spread focuses on a single skill.

Concise text introduces the basic principles in the lesson and integrates a real-world case study.

## Saving a Presentation

UNIT
A
PowerPoint 2003

To store your presentation so that you can work on it or view it again at a later time, you must save it as a **file** on a disk. When you first save a presentation, you give it a name, called a **filename**, and determine the location where you want to store the file. After you initially save your presentation, you should then save your presentation periodically as you continue to work so that any changes are saved in the file. As a general rule, it's wise to save your work about every 5 to 10 minutes and before printing. You use either the Save command or the Save As command on the File menu to save your presentation for the first time. When you want to make a copy of an existing presentation using a different name, use the Save As command; otherwise, use the Save command to save your changes to a presentation file. Save your presentation as Marketing Campaign.

### STEPS

1. **Click File on the menu bar, then click** Save As
   The Save As dialog box opens, similar to Figure A-10. See Table A-3 for a description of the Save As dialog box button functions.

2. **Click the** Save in list arrow, **then navigate to the drive and folder where your Data Files are stored**
   A default filename, which PowerPoint creates from the presentation title you entered, appears in the File name text box. If the selected drive or folder contains any PowerPoint files, their filenames appear in the white area in the center of the dialog box.

3. **Click** Save
   Filenames can be up to 255 characters long; you may use lowercase or uppercase letters, symbols, numbers, and spaces. The Save As dialog box closes, and the new filename appears in the title bar at the top of the Presentation window. PowerPoint remembers which view your presentation is in when you save it, so you decide to save the presentation in Normal view instead of Notes Page view.

4. **Click the** Normal View button 
   The presentation view changes from Notes Page view to Normal view as shown in Figure A-11.

   **QUICK TIP**
   To save a file quickly, you can press the shortcut key combination [Ctrl][S].

5. **Click the** Save button  **on the Standard toolbar**
   The Save command saves any changes you made to the file to the same location you specified when you used the Save As command. Save your file frequently while working with it to protect your presentation.

### Clues to Use

**Saving fonts with your presentation**
When you create a presentation, it uses the fonts that are installed on your computer. If you need to open the presentation on another computer, the fonts might look different if that computer has a different set of fonts. To preserve the look of your presentation on any computer, you can save, or embed, the fonts in your presentation. Click File on the menu bar, then click Save As. The Save As dialog box opens. Click Tools, click Save Options, then click the Embed TrueType fonts check box in the Save Options dialog box. Click OK to close the Save Options dialog box, then click Save. Now the presentation looks the same on any computer that opens it. Using this option, however, significantly increases the size of your presentation on disk, so only use it when necessary. You can freely embed any TrueType font that comes with Windows. You can embed other TrueType fonts only if they have no license restrictions.

POWERPOINT A-12 GETTING STARTED WITH POWERPOINT 2003

OFFICE–448

Hints, as well as troubleshooting advice, are located right where you need them—next to the step itself.

Clues to Use boxes provide concise information that either expands on the major lesson skill or describes an independent task that in some way relates to the major lesson skill.

Every lesson features large, full-color representations of what the screen should look like as students complete the numbered steps.

## What online content solutions are available to accompany this book?

Visit www.course.com for more information on our online content for Illustrated titles. Options include:

### MyCourse 2.0
Need a quick, simple tool to help you manage your course? Try MyCourse 2.0, the easiest to use, most flexible syllabus and content management tool available. MyCourse 2.0 offers you brand new content, including Topic Reviews, Extra Case Projects, and Quizzes, to accompany this book.

### WebCT
Thomson Course Technology and WebCT have partnered to provide you with the highest quality online resources and Web-based tools for your class. Thomson Course Technology offers content for this book to help you create your WebCT class, such as a suggested Syllabus, Lecture Notes, Practice Test questions, and more.

### Blackboard
Thomson Course Technology and Blackboard have also partnered to provide you with the highest quality online resources and Web-based tools for your class. Thomson Course Technology offers content for this book to help you create your Blackboard class, such as a suggested Syllabus, Lecture Notes, Practice Test questions, and more.

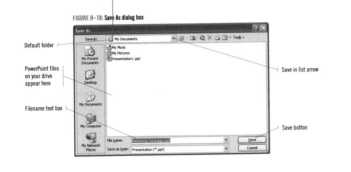

FIGURE A-10: Save As dialog box

Default folder

PowerPoint files on your drive appear here

Filename text box

Save in list arrow

Save button

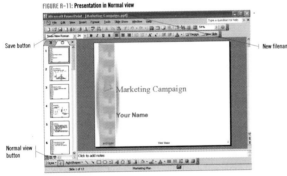

FIGURE A-11: Presentation in Normal view

Save button

Normal view button

New filename

**PowerPoint 2003**

TABLE A-3: Save As dialog box button functions

| button | button name | used to |
|---|---|---|
| | Back | Navigate to the drive or folder previously displayed in the Save in list box |
| | Up One Level | Navigate to the next highest level in the folder hierarchy |
| | Search the Web | Connect to the World Wide Web |
| | Delete | Delete the selected folder or file |
| | Create New Folder | Create a new folder in the current folder or drive |
| | Views | Change the way folders and files are viewed in the dialog box |
| Tools ▾ | Tools | Open a menu of commands to help you work with selected files and folders |

GETTING STARTED WITH POWERPOINT 2003 POWERPOINT A-13

Tables provide quickly accessible summaries of key terms, toolbar buttons, or keyboard alternatives connected with the lesson material. Students can refer easily to this information when working on their own projects at a later time.

The pages are numbered according to application and unit. PowerPoint indicates the application, A indicates the unit, 13 indicates the page.

# Instructor Resources

The Instructor Resources CD is Course Technology's way of putting the resources and information needed to teach and learn effectively into your hands. With an integrated array of teaching and learning tools that offers you and your students a broad range of technology-based instructional options, we believe this CD represents the highest quality and most cutting edge resources available to instructors today. Many of these resources are available at www.course.com. The resources available with this book are:

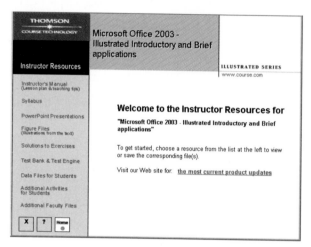

- **Data Files for Students**—To complete most of the units in this book, your students will need **Data Files**. Put them on a file server for students to copy. The Data Files are available on the Instructor Resources CD-ROM, in the Review Pack, and can also be downloaded from www.course.com.

  Instruct students to use the **Data Files List** located in the Review Pack and on the Instructor Resources CD. This list gives instructions on copying and organizing files.

- **Solutions to Exercises**—Solutions to Exercises contains every file students are asked to create or modify in the lessons and End-of-Unit material. A Help file on the Instructor Resources CD includes information for using the Solution Files. There is also a document outlining the solutions for the End-of-Unit Concepts Reviews, Skills Reviews, and Independent Challenges.

- **PowerPoint Presentations**—Each unit has a corresponding PowerPoint presentation that you can use in lecture, distribute to your students, or customize to suit your course.

- **Instructor's Manual**—Available as an electronic file, the Instructor's Manual is quality-assurance tested and includes unit overviews, detailed lecture topics with teaching tips for each unit.

- **Sample Syllabus**—Prepare and customize your course easily using this sample course outline.

- **ExamView**—ExamView is a powerful testing software package that allows you to create and administer printed, computer (LAN-based), and Internet exams. ExamView includes hundreds of questions that correspond to the topics covered in this text, enabling students to generate detailed study guides that include page references for further review. The computer-based and Internet testing components allow students to take exams at their computers, and also saves you time by grading each exam automatically.

- **Figure Files**—The figures in the text are provided on the Instructor Resources CD to help you illustrate key topics or concepts. You can create traditional overhead transparencies by printing the figure files. Or you can create electronic slide shows by using the figures in a presentation program such as PowerPoint.

## SAM 2003 Assessment & Training

SAM 2003 helps you energize your class exams and training assignments by allowing students to learn and test important computer skills in an active, hands-on environment.

With SAM 2003 Assessment, you create powerful interactive exams on critical applications such as Word, Outlook, PowerPoint, Windows, the Internet, and much more. The exams simulate the application environment, allowing your students to demonstrate their knowledge and think through the skill by performing real-world tasks.

Designed to be used with the Illustrated series, SAM 2003 Assessment & Training includes built-in page references so students can create study guides that match the Illustrated textbooks you use in class. Powerful administrative options allow you to schedule exams and assignments, secure your tests, and run reports with almost limitless flexibility.

# Contents

Preface ...............................................................................................iv

## POWERPOINT 2003

### Getting Started with PowerPoint 2003          A-1

Defining Presentation Software .........................................A-2
Starting PowerPoint 2003 .................................................A-4
    Creating a PowerPoint shortcut on the desktop
Viewing the PowerPoint Window.......................................A-6
    Toolbars and menus in PowerPoint 2003
Using the AutoContent Wizard .........................................A-8
    About wizards and the PowerPoint installation
Viewing a Presentation ...................................................A-10
Saving a Presentation .....................................................A-12
    Saving fonts with your presentation
Getting Help and Researching Information .....................A-14
    Recovering lost presentation files
Printing and Closing the File, and Exiting PowerPoint ...........A-16
    Viewing your presentation in grayscale or black and white
Concepts Review .............................................................A-18
Skills Review ..................................................................A-20
Independent Challenges ..................................................A-21
Visual Workshop .............................................................A-24

## POWERPOINT 2003

### Creating a Presentation          B-1

Planning an Effective Presentation ...................................B-2
    Using templates from the Web
Entering Slide Text...........................................................B-4
    Using Speech Recognition
Creating a New Slide ........................................................B-6
Entering Text in the Outline Tab ......................................B-8
    What do I do if I see a lightbulb on a slide?
Adding Slide Headers and Footers....................................B-10
    Entering and printing notes
Choosing a Look for a Presentation .................................B-12
    Using design templates
Checking Spelling in a Presentation .................................B-14
    Checking spelling as you type
Evaluating a Presentation ...............................................B-16
Concepts Review .............................................................B-18
Skills Review ..................................................................B-19
Independent Challenges ..................................................B-21
Visual Workshop .............................................................B-24

## POWERPOINT 2003

### Modifying a Presentation          C-1

Opening an Existing Presentation .....................................C-2
    Setting permissions
Drawing and Modifying an Object.....................................C-4
    Understanding PowerPoint objects
Editing Drawn Objects .....................................................C-6
    More ways to change objects
Aligning and Grouping Objects .........................................C-8
Adding and Arranging Text ............................................C-10
    Review a presentation
Formatting Text..............................................................C-12
    Replacing text and attributes
Importing Text from Microsoft Word...............................C-14
    Inserting slides from other presentations
Customizing the Color Scheme and Background ..................C-16
Concepts Review .............................................................C-18
Skills Review ..................................................................C-20
Independent Challenges ..................................................C-22
Visual Workshop .............................................................C-24

## POWERPOINT 2003

### Enhancing a Presentation          D-1

Inserting Clip Art ...........................................................D-2
    Find more clips online
Inserting, Cropping, and Scaling a Picture.......................D-4
    Using graphics in PowerPoint
Embedding a Chart..........................................................D-6
Entering and Editing Data in the Datasheet .....................D-8
    Series in Rows vs. Series in Columns
Formatting a Chart ........................................................D-10
    Customizing data series in charts
Creating Tables in PowerPoint .......................................D-12
Using Slide Show Commands...........................................D-14
Setting Slide Show Timings and Transitions ...................D-16
    Rehearsing slide show timing
Setting Slide Animation Effects ......................................D-18
    Presentation checklist
Concepts Review .............................................................D-20
Skills Review ..................................................................D-21
Independent Challenges...................................................D-22
Visual Workshop.............................................................D-24

# Read This Before You Begin

## Software Information and Required Installation

This book was written and tested using Microsoft Office 2003 - Professional Edition, with a typical installation on Microsoft Windows XP, including installation of the most recent Windows XP Service Pack, and with Internet Explorer 6.0 or higher. Some of the exercises in this book assume that your computer is connected to the Internet. If you are not connected to the Internet, see your instructor.

## Tips for Students

### What are Data Files?

To complete many of the units in this book, you need to use Data Files. A Data File contains a partially completed presentation file, so that you don't have to type in all the information yourself. Your instructor will either provide you with copies of the Data Files or ask you to make your own copies. Your instructor can also give you instructions on how to organize your files, as well as a complete file listing, or you can find the list and the instructions for organizing your files in the Review Pack. In addition, because there are no Data Files supplied for Unit A or Unit B, you will need to create folders for Units A and B at the same level as your other unit folders in order to save the files you create.

### Why is my screen different from the book?

Your desktop components and some dialog box options might be different if you are using an operating system other than Windows XP.

Depending on your computer hardware and the Display settings on your computer, you may also notice the following differences:

• Your screen may look larger or smaller because of your screen resolution (the height and width of your screen).

• Your title bars and dialog boxes may not display file extensions. To display file extensions, click Start on the taskbar, click Control Panel, click Appearance and Themes, then click Folder Options. Click the View tab if necessary, click Hide extensions for known file types to deselect it, then click OK. Your Office dialog boxes and title bars should now display file extensions.

• Depending on your Office settings, your toolbars may be displayed on a single row and your menus may display a shortened list of frequently used commands. Office menus and toolbars can modify themselves to your working style by displaying only the most frequently used buttons and menu commands, as shown here.

### Toolbars in one row

### Toolbars in two rows

To view buttons not currently displayed, click a Toolbar Options button ⁀ at the end of either the Standard or Formatting toolbar. To view the full list of menu commands, click the double arrow at the bottom of the menu.

In order to have your toolbars displayed in two rows, showing all buttons, and to have the full menus displayed, you must turn off the personalized menus and toolbars feature. Click Tools on the menu bar, click Customize, select the show Standard and Formatting toolbars on two rows and Always show full menus check boxes on the Options tab, and then click Close. This book assumes you are displaying toolbars in two rows and displaying full menus.

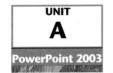

# Getting Started with PowerPoint 2003

## OBJECTIVES

| Define presentation software |
| Start PowerPoint 2003 |
| View the PowerPoint window |
| Use the AutoContent Wizard |
| View a presentation |
| Save a presentation |
| Get Help and research information |
| Print and close the file, and exit PowerPoint 2003 |

If you have a SAM user profile, you may have access to hands-on instruction, practice, and assessment of the skills covered in this unit. Log in to your SAM account and go to your assignments page to see what your instructor has assigned.

Microsoft Office PowerPoint 2003 is a computer program that enables you to create visually compelling presentations. With PowerPoint, you can create individual slides and display them as a slide show on your computer, video projector, or even via the Internet. Maria Abbott is the general sales manager at MediaLoft, a chain of bookstore cafés founded in 1988. MediaLoft stores offer customers the opportunity to purchase books, music, and movies while enjoying a variety of coffees, teas, and freshly baked desserts. As her assistant, Maria needs you to learn the basics of PowerPoint so you can create presentations for the sales department.

# Defining Presentation Software

**Presentation software** is a computer program you can use to organize and present information and ideas. Whether you are giving a sales pitch or explaining your company's goals and accomplishments, presentation software can help you communicate effectively and professionally. You can use PowerPoint to create presentations, as well as notes for the presenter and handouts for the audience. Table A-1 explains the items you can create using PowerPoint. 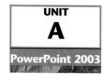 Maria wants you to create a presentation that explains a new marketing campaign that the MediaLoft Sales Department is developing. Because you are not that familiar with PowerPoint, you get to work exploring its capabilities. Figure A-1 shows a handout you created using a word processor for a recent presentation. Figure A-2 shows how the information might look in PowerPoint.

## DETAILS

### You can easily complete the following tasks using PowerPoint:

- **Present information in a variety of ways**

  With PowerPoint, you can present information using a variety of methods. For example, you can print handout pages or an outline of your presentation for your audience. You can display your presentation as an electronic slide show on a computer. If you are presenting to a large group in a conference room, you can use a video projector. If you want to reach an even wider audience, you can post your presentation so it can be viewed over the Internet.

- **Enter and edit data easily**

  Using PowerPoint, you can enter and edit data quickly and efficiently. When you need to change a part of your presentation, you can use the word processing and outlining capabilities of PowerPoint to edit your content rather than re-create it.

- **Change the appearance of information**

  PowerPoint has many features that can transform the way text, graphics, and slides appear. By exploring some of these capabilities, you discover how easy it is to change the appearance of your presentation.

- **Organize and arrange information**

  Once you start using PowerPoint, you won't have to spend much time making sure your information is correct and in the right order. With PowerPoint, you can quickly and easily rearrange and modify text, graphics, and slides in your presentation.

- **Incorporate information from other sources**

  Often, when you create presentations, you use information from other sources. With PowerPoint, you can import text, graphics, and numerical data from spreadsheet, database, and word processing files such as Microsoft Excel, Microsoft Access, Microsoft Word, and Corel WordPerfect. You can also import graphic images from a variety of sources such as the Internet, image files on a computer, or other graphics programs. Likewise, you can also incorporate changes made to your presentation by others who review it.

- **Show a presentation on any computer that doesn't have PowerPoint installed**

  By using the Package for CD feature, you can copy your presentation and its supporting files to a CD to be viewed on another computer, even if the computer doesn't have PowerPoint installed. The PowerPoint Viewer, which is included on the CD when you package a presentation, displays a presentation as an on-screen slide show on any compatible computer. To package a presentation directly to a CD, your computer must be running Windows XP or later.

1 Marketing Campaign
  Your Name

2 Market Summary
  • Market: past, present, & future
    – Review changes in market share, leadership, players, market shifts, costs, pricing, competition

3 Product Definition
  • Describe product/service being marketed

4 Competition
  • The competitive landscape
    – Provide an overview of product competitors, their strengths and weaknesses
    – Position each competitor's product against new product

5 Positioning
  • Positioning of product or service
    – Statement that distinctly defines the product in its market and against its competition over time
  • Consumer promise
    – Statement summarizing the benefit of the product or service to the consumer

6 Communication Strategies
  • Messaging by audience
  • Target consumer demographics

7 Packaging & Fulfillment
  • Product packaging
    – Discuss form-factor, pricing, look, strategy
    – Discuss fulfillment issues for items not shipped directly with product
  • COGs
    – Summarize Cost of Goods and high-level Bill of Materials

8 Launch Strategies
  • Launch plan
    – If product is being announced
  • Promotion budget
    – Supply back up material with detailed budget information for review

9 Public Relations
  • Strategy & execution
    – PR strategies
    – PR plan highlights

1

FIGURE A-2: PowerPoint handout

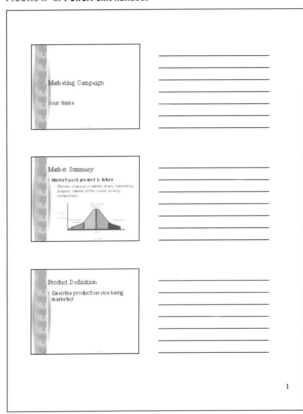

TABLE A-1: Presenting information using PowerPoint

| item | use |
| --- | --- |
| On-screen presentations | Run a slide show directly from your computer |
| Web presentations | Broadcast a presentation on the Web or on an intranet that others can view, complete with video and audio |
| Online meetings | View or work on a presentation with your colleagues in real time |
| Color overheads | Print PowerPoint slides directly to transparencies on your color printer |
| Black-and-white overheads | Print PowerPoint slides directly to transparencies on your black-and-white printer |
| Notes | Print notes that help you remember points about each slide when you speak to a group |
| Audience handouts | Print handouts with two, three, or six slides on a page |
| Outline pages | Print the outline of your presentation to highlight the main points |

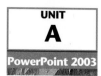

# Starting PowerPoint 2003

To start PowerPoint 2003, you must first start Windows. You have to click the Start button on the taskbar, then point to All Programs to display the All Programs menu. Point to Microsoft Office to open the Microsoft Office menu which contains the Microsoft PowerPoint program name and icon. If Microsoft PowerPoint is not in the All Programs menu, it might be in a different location on your computer. If you are using a computer on a network, you might need to use a different starting procedure. ▰▰▰▰ Start PowerPoint to familiarize yourself with the program.

## STEPS

1. **Make sure your computer is on and the Windows desktop is visible**
   If any program windows are open, close or minimize them.

2. **Click the Start button ❚ start on the taskbar, point to All Programs**
   The All Programs menu opens, showing a list of icons and names for all your programs.

3. **Point to Microsoft Office**
   You see the Microsoft Office programs installed on your computer, as shown in Figure A-3. Your screen might look different, depending on which programs are installed on your computer.

> **TROUBLE**
> If you have trouble finding Microsoft PowerPoint on the Programs menu, check with your instructor or technical support person.

4. **Click Microsoft Office PowerPoint 2003 on the Microsoft Office menu**
   PowerPoint starts, and the PowerPoint window opens, as shown in Figure A-4.

## Clues to Use

### Creating a PowerPoint shortcut on the desktop

You can make it easier to start PowerPoint by placing a shortcut on the desktop. To create the shortcut, click the Start button ❚ start, then point to All Programs. On the All Programs menu, point to Microsoft Office, point to Microsoft Office PowerPoint, then right-click Microsoft Office PowerPoint 2003. In the shortcut menu that appears, point to Send To, then click Desktop (create shortcut). Windows places a Microsoft PowerPoint shortcut icon on your desktop. In the future, you can start PowerPoint by simply double-clicking this icon, instead of using the Start menu. You can edit or change the name of the shortcut by right-clicking the shortcut icon, clicking Rename on the shortcut menu, and then typing a new name as you would name any item in Windows. If you are working in a computer lab, you may not be allowed to place shortcuts on the desktop. Check with your instructor or technical support person before attempting to add a shortcut.

**FIGURE A-3:** All Programs menu

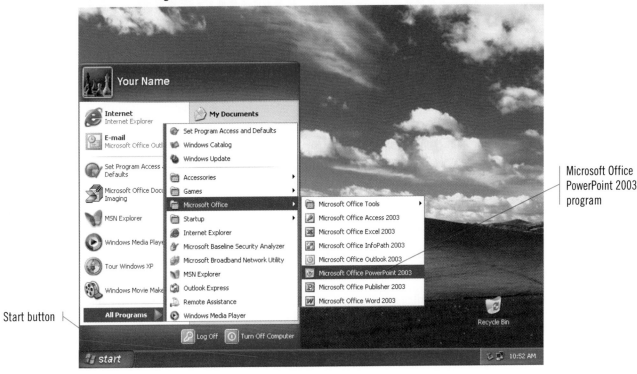

Start button

Microsoft Office
PowerPoint 2003
program

**FIGURE A-4:** PowerPoint window

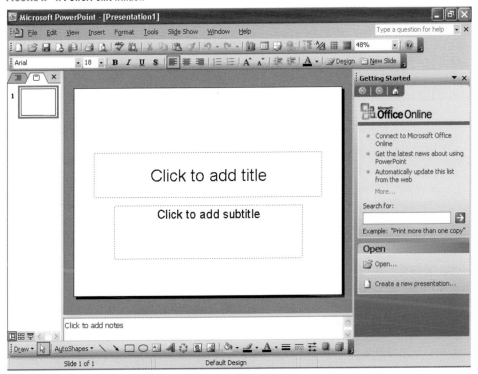

PowerPoint 2003

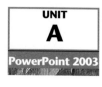

# Viewing the PowerPoint Window

When you first start PowerPoint, a blank slide appears in the PowerPoint window. PowerPoint has different **views** that allow you to see your presentation in different forms. By default, the PowerPoint window opens in **Normal view**, which is the primary view that you use to write, edit, and design your presentation. Normal view is divided into three areas called **panes**: the pane on the left contains the Outline and Slides tabs, the Slide pane, and the notes pane. You move around in each pane using the scroll bars. The PowerPoint window and the specific parts of the Normal view are described below.

## DETAILS

**Using Figure A-5 as a guide, examine the elements of the PowerPoint window, then find and compare the elements described below:**

- The **title bar** contains a program Control Menu button, the program name, the title of the presentation, resizing buttons, and the program Close button.

- The **menu bar** contains the names of the menus you use to choose PowerPoint commands, as well as the Type a question for help box and the Close Window button.

- The **Standard toolbar** contains buttons for commonly used commands, such as copying and pasting. The **Formatting toolbar** contains buttons for the most frequently used formatting commands, such as changing font type and size. The toolbars on your screen may be displayed on one line instead of two. See the Clues to Use for more information on how toolbars are displayed.

- The **Outline tab** displays your presentation text in the form of an outline, without graphics. In this tab, it is easy to move text on or among slides by dragging text to reorder the information.

- The **Slides tab** displays the slides of your presentation as small images, called **thumbnails**. You can quickly navigate through the slides in your presentation by clicking the thumbnails on this tab. You can also add, delete, or rearrange slides using this tab.

- The **Slide pane** displays the current slide in your presentation, including all text and graphics.

- The **notes pane** is used to type notes that reference a slide's content. You can print these notes and refer to them when you make a presentation or print them as handouts and give them to your audience. The notes pane is not visible to the audience when you show a slide presentation in Slide Show view.

- The **task pane** contains sets of hyperlinks for commonly used commands. The commands are grouped into 16 different task panes. The commands include creating new presentations, opening existing presentations, searching for documents, and using the Office Clipboard. You can also perform basic formatting tasks from the task pane such as changing the slide layout, slide design, color scheme, or slide animations of a presentation.

- The **Drawing toolbar**, located at the bottom of the PowerPoint window, contains buttons and menus that let you create lines, shapes, and special effects.

- The **view buttons**, at the bottom of the Outline tab and Slides tab area, allow you to quickly switch between PowerPoint views.

- The **status bar**, located at the bottom of the PowerPoint window, shows messages about what you are doing and seeing in PowerPoint, including which slide you are viewing.

**FIGURE A-5:** Presentation window in Normal view

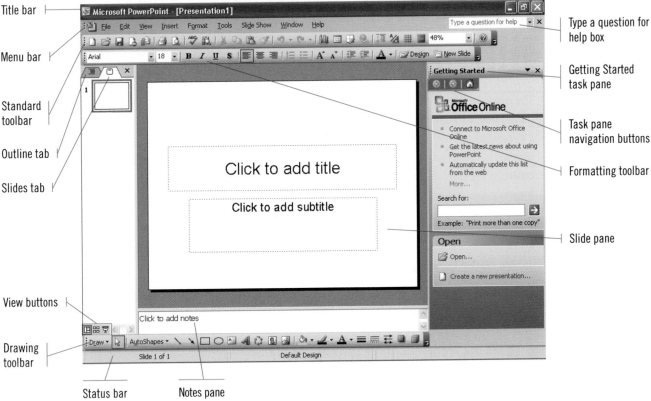

Title bar
Menu bar
Standard toolbar
Outline tab
Slides tab
View buttons
Drawing toolbar
Status bar
Notes pane

Type a question for help box
Getting Started task pane
Task pane navigation buttons
Formatting toolbar
Slide pane

PowerPoint 2003

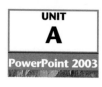
# Using the AutoContent Wizard

The quickest way to create a presentation is with the AutoContent Wizard. A **wizard** is a series of steps that guides you through a task (in this case, creating a presentation). Using the AutoContent Wizard, you choose a presentation type from the wizard's list of sample presentations. Then you indicate what type of output you want. Next, you type the information for the title slide and the footer. The AutoContent Wizard then creates a presentation with sample text you can use as a guide to help formulate the major points of your presentation. ▨▨▨ You decide to start your presentation by opening the AutoContent Wizard.

## STEPS

**QUICK TIP**
You can also access the New Presentation task pane by clicking Create a new presentation in the Open section on the Getting Started task pane.

1. **Click the** Other Task Panes list arrow ▼ **in the task pane title bar, then click** New Presentation
   The New Presentation task pane opens.

2. **Point to the** From AutoContent wizard hyperlink **in the New section of the task pane**
   The mouse pointer changes to the Hyperlink pointer 🖑. The pointer changes to this shape any time it is positioned over a hyperlink.

3. **Click the** From AutoContent wizard hyperlink
   The AutoContent Wizard dialog box opens, as shown in Figure A-6. The left section of the dialog box outlines the contents of the AutoContent Wizard, and the text in the right section explains the current wizard screen.

4. **Click** Next
   The Presentation type screen appears. This screen contains category buttons and types of presentations. Each presentation type contains suggested text for a particular use. By default, the presentation types in the General category are listed.

5. **Click the** Sales/Marketing **category, click** Marketing Plan **in the list on the right, then click** Next
   The Presentation style screen appears, asking you to choose an output type. The On-screen presentation option is selected by default.

6. **Click** Next, **click in the** Presentation title text box, **then type** Marketing Campaign
   The Presentation options screen requests information that appears on the title slide of the presentation and in the footer at the bottom of each slide. The Date last updated and the Slide number check boxes are selected by default.

7. **Press** [Tab], **then type** Your Name **in the Footer text box**

8. **Click** Next, **then click** Finish
   The AutoContent Wizard opens the presentation based on the Marketing Plan presentation type you chose. Sample text for each slide is listed on the left in the Outline tab, and the title slide appears in the Slide pane on the right side of the screen. Notice that the task pane is no longer visible. The task pane can be easily opened the next time you need it. Compare your screen to Figure A-7.

**FIGURE A-6:** AutoContent Wizard opening screen

The green box identifies which step you are completing

**FIGURE A-7:** Presentation created with AutoContent Wizard

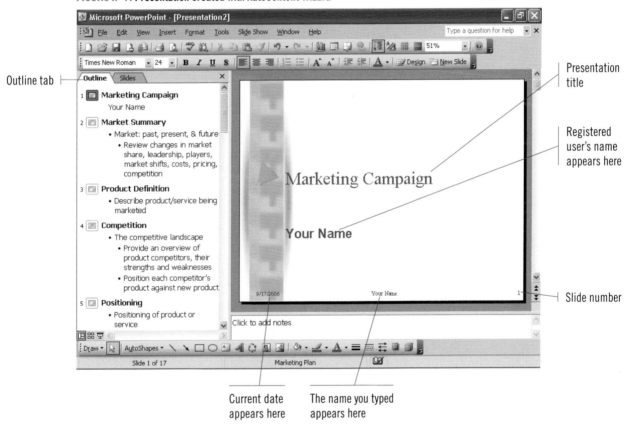

Outline tab

Current date appears here

The name you typed appears here

Presentation title

Registered user's name appears here

Slide number

### Clues to Use

## About wizards and the PowerPoint installation

As you use PowerPoint, you may find that not all AutoContent Wizards are available to you. The wizards that are available depend on your PowerPoint installation. A typical installation of PowerPoint provides you with many wizards, templates, and other features. However, some features may require you to run an install program before you use the feature for the first time. If you find a feature that is not installed, run the install program as directed. In some instances you may be required to insert the Office CD in order to install a feature. If you are working on a networked computer or in a lab, see your technical support person for assistance.

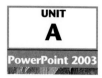

# Viewing a Presentation

This lesson introduces you to the four PowerPoint views: Normal view, Slide Sorter view, Slide Show view, and Notes Page view. Each PowerPoint view shows your presentation in a different way and allows you to manipulate your presentation differently. To move easily among most of the PowerPoint views, use the view buttons located at the bottom of the pane containing the Outline and Slides tabs. Table A-2 provides a brief description of the PowerPoint views. Examine each of the PowerPoint views, starting with Normal view.

## STEPS

1. **In the Outline tab, click the small slide icon next to Slide 4**

    The text for Slide 4 is selected in the Outline tab and Slide 4 appears in the Slide pane as shown in Figure A-8. Notice that the status bar also indicates the number of the slide you are viewing, the total number of slides in the presentation, and the name of the AutoContent wizard you are using.

2. **Click the Previous Slide button at the bottom of the vertical scroll bar three times so that Slide 1 (the title slide) appears**

    The scroll box in the vertical scroll bar moves back up the scroll bar. The gray slide icon on the Outline tab indicates which slide is displayed in the Slide pane. As you scroll through the presentation, read the sample text on each slide created by the AutoContent Wizard.

3. **Click the Slides tab**

    Thumbnails of all the slides in your presentation appear on the Slides tab and the Slide pane enlarges.

4. **Click the Slide Sorter View button**

    A thumbnail of each slide in the presentation appears as shown in Figure A-9. You can examine the flow of your slides and drag any slide or group of slides to rearrange the order of the slides in the presentation.

5. **Double-click the first slide in Slide Sorter view**

    The slide appears in Normal view. The Slide pane shows the selected slide.

6. **Click the Slide Show from current slide button**

    The first slide fills the entire screen. In this view, you can practice running through your slides as they would appear in the slide show.

7. **Press the left mouse button, press [Enter], or press [Spacebar] to advance through the slides one at a time until you see a black slide, then click once more to return to Normal view**

    The black slide at the end of the slide show indicates that the slide show is finished. When you click the black slide (or press [Spacebar] or [Enter]), you automatically return to the slide and view you were in before you ran the slide show, in this case Slide 1 in Normal view.

> **TROUBLE**
> If you don't see a menu command, click the Expand button at the bottom of the menu.

8. **Click View on the menu bar, then click Notes Page**

    Notes Page view appears, showing a reduced image of the current slide above a large text box. You can enter text in this box and then print the notes page for your own use to help you remember important points about your presentation. To switch to Notes Page view, you must choose Notes Page from the View menu; there is no Notes Page view button.

**FIGURE A-8: Normal view with the Outline tab displayed**

Slides tab

Slide icon

Slide Show from current slide button

Slide Sorter View button

Normal View button

Current slide number and total number of slides

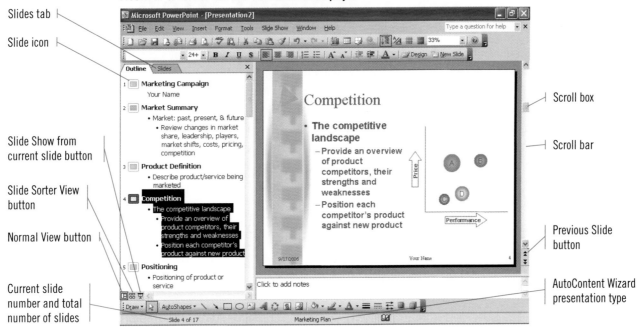

Scroll box

Scroll bar

Previous Slide button

AutoContent Wizard presentation type

**FIGURE A-9: Slide Sorter view**

Step 5

Slide Sorter View button

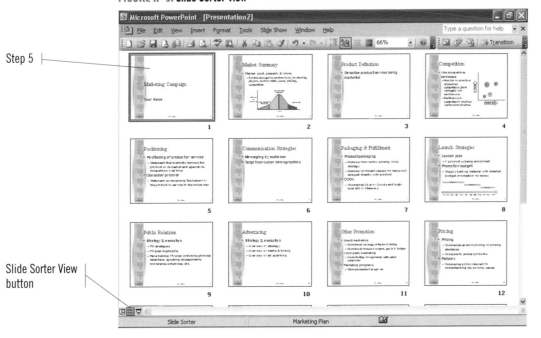

**TABLE A-2: PowerPoint views**

| view name | button | button name | description |
|---|---|---|---|
| Normal |  | Normal View | Displays the pane that contains the Outline and Slides tabs, Slide pane, and notes panes at the same time; use this view to work on your presentation's content, layout, and notes concurrently |
| Slide Sorter | | Slide Sorter View | Displays thumbnails of all slides in the order in which they appear in your presentation; use this view to rearrange and add special effects to your slides |
| Slide Show | | Slide Show from current slide | Displays your presentation as an electronic slide show |
| Notes Page | | | Displays a reduced image of the current slide above a large text box where you can enter or view notes |

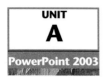

# Saving a Presentation

To store your presentation so that you can work on it or view it again at a later time, you must save it as a **file** on a disk. When you first save a presentation, you give it a name, called a **filename**, and determine the location where you want to store the file. After you initially save your presentation, you should then save your presentation periodically as you continue to work so that any changes are saved in the file. As a general rule, it's wise to save your work about every 5 to 10 minutes and before printing. You use either the Save command or the Save As command on the File menu to save your presentation for the first time. When you want to make a copy of an existing presentation using a different name, use the Save As command; otherwise, use the Save command to save your changes to a presentation file.   Save your presentation as Marketing Campaign.

**STEPS**

1. **Click File on the menu bar, then click Save As**

   The Save As dialog box opens, similar to Figure A-10. See Table A-3 for a description of the Save As dialog box button functions.

2. **Click the Save in list arrow, then navigate to the drive and folder where your Data Files are stored**

   A default filename, which PowerPoint creates from the presentation title you entered, appears in the File name text box. If the selected drive or folder contains any PowerPoint files, their filenames appear in the white area in the center of the dialog box.

3. **Click Save**

   Filenames can be up to 255 characters long; you may use lowercase or uppercase letters, symbols, numbers, and spaces. The Save As dialog box closes, and the new filename appears in the title bar at the top of the Presentation window. PowerPoint remembers which view your presentation is in when you save it, so you decide to save the presentation in Normal view instead of Notes Page view.

4. **Click the Normal View button** ▣

   The presentation view changes from Notes Page view to Normal view as shown in Figure A-11.

**QUICK TIP**
To save a file quickly, you can press the shortcut key combination [Ctrl][S].

5. **Click the Save button** 🖫 **on the Standard toolbar**

   The Save command saves any changes you made to the file to the same location you specified when you used the Save As command. Save your file frequently while working with it to protect your presentation.

---

### Clues to Use

#### Saving fonts with your presentation

When you create a presentation, it uses the fonts that are installed on your computer. If you need to open the presentation on another computer, the fonts might look different if that computer has a different set of fonts. To preserve the look of your presentation on any computer, you can save, or embed, the fonts in your presentation. Click File on the menu bar, then click Save As. The Save As dialog box opens. Click Tools, click Save Options, then click the Embed TrueType fonts check box in the Save Options dialog box. Click OK to close the Save Options dialog box, then click Save. Now the presentation looks the same on any computer that opens it. Using this option, however, significantly increases the size of your presentation on disk, so only use it when necessary. You can freely embed any TrueType font that comes with Windows. You can embed other TrueType fonts only if they have no license restrictions.

**FIGURE A-10:** Save As dialog box

Default folder

PowerPoint files on your drive appear here

Filename text box

Save in list arrow

Save button

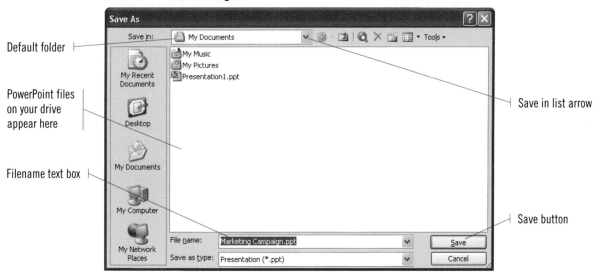

**FIGURE A-11:** Presentation in Normal view

Save button

New filename

Normal view button

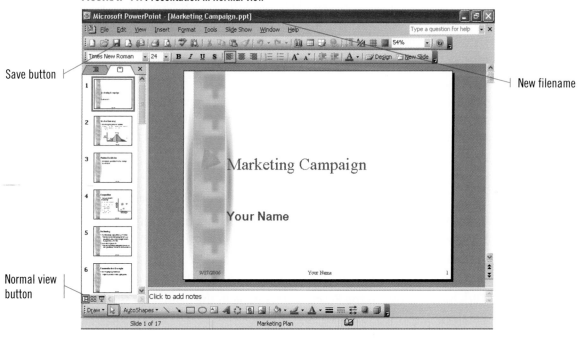

**TABLE A-3:** Save As dialog box button functions

| button | button name | used to |
|--------|-------------|---------|
| | Back | Navigate to the drive or folder previously displayed in the Save in list box |
| | Up One Level | Navigate to the next highest level in the folder hierarchy |
| | Search the Web | Connect to the World Wide Web |
| | Delete | Delete the selected folder or file |
| | Create New Folder | Create a new folder in the current folder or drive |
| | Views | Change the way folders and files are viewed in the dialog box |
| Tools ▾ | Tools | Open a menu of commands to help you work with selected files and folders |

PowerPoint 2003

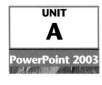

# Getting Help and Researching Information

PowerPoint has an extensive Help system that gives you immediate access to program definitions, reference information, and feature explanations. To access Help information, you can type a word, phrase, or question in the Type a question for help box on the menu bar or you can click the Help button on the Standard toolbar. Help information appears in a separate window that you can move and resize. You can also access other resources such as dictionaries, thesauruses, or Web sites to research information on various topics related to PowerPoint. If the information you are looking for does not appear in the Help window, you can rephrase your question and try your search again. You are finished working on your presentation for now and you decide to learn about hyperlinks.

## STEPS

**TROUBLE**
If your search results are not from www.microsoft.com, then you may not be connected to the Internet. Check with your instructor or technical support person for help. If you are unable to connect to the Internet, you will not be able to complete all of the steps in this lesson.

1. **Click in the Type a question for help box on the menu bar, type hyperlinks, then press [Enter]**
   The Search Results task pane appears showing Help topics related to hyperlinks. See Figure A-12.

2. **If necessary, click the down scroll arrow in the Search Results task pane, then click the About hyperlinks and action buttons hyperlink in the results list**
   The Microsoft PowerPoint Help window opens and displays information about hyperlinks and action buttons.

3. **Click the down scroll arrow on the vertical scroll bar in the Help window to read all of the Help information**
   Notice the hyperlinks (blue words) in the Help text, which you can click to get further information on that particular subject. Two subtopic hyperlinks, which are identified by small blue arrows, are below the Help information. To view information on either of these topics, simply click the topic hyperlink.

4. **Click the Testing and repairing broken hyperlinks subtopic, click the down scroll arrow, then read the information**
   Notice that the small blue arrow now points down indicating that the subtopic is displayed.

**TROUBLE**
A dialog box may open telling you that the Research feature is not installed. Install the Research feature using the Office CD or check with your instructor or technical support person for help.

5. **Click the Other Task Panes list arrow ▼ in the task pane title bar, click Research, click in the Search for text box, type hyperlinks, then click the Start searching button →**
   The Research task pane displays information found in the default research Web sites and reference books. Figure A-13 shows the Research task pane with the results of the research on the term 'hyperlinks'.

6. **Click the list arrow in the Research task pane in the Search for section, then click All Research Sites**
   PowerPoint researches the currently available Web sites for information on hyperlinks and displays the information in the Research task pane. To further help your ability to research topics, PowerPoint allows you to choose which reference books, research Web sites, and other research services you can use when doing research.

7. **Click the Close button ☒ in the Microsoft PowerPoint Help window title bar**
   The Help window closes, and your presentation fills the screen again. The Research task pane should still be visible.

8. **Click the Research options hyperlink at the bottom of the Research task pane**
   The Research Options dialog box opens. The options in this dialog box allow you to customize the tools that will be used to research information.

9. **Click the down scroll arrow in the dialog box to view all of the available options, then click Cancel**

**FIGURE A-12:** Search Results task pane showing Help topics

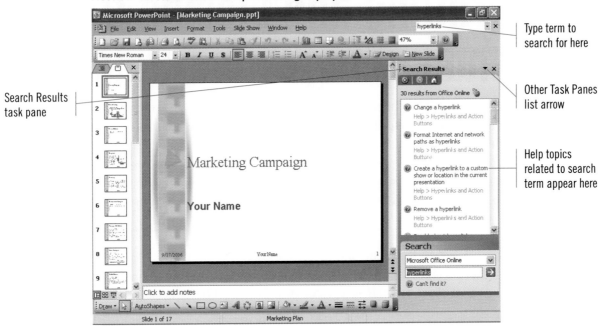

Search Results task pane

Type term to search for here

Other Task Panes list arrow

Help topics related to search term appear here

**FIGURE A-13:** PowerPoint window showing Research task pane

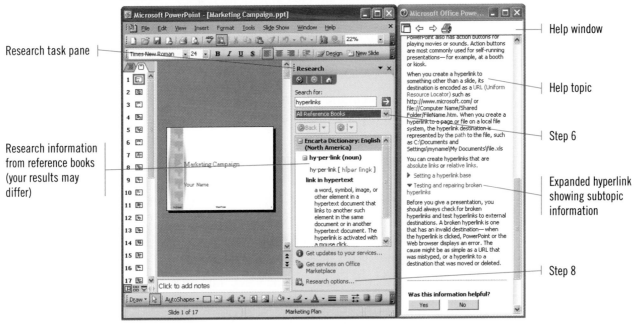

Research task pane

Research information from reference books (your results may differ)

Help window

Help topic

Step 6

Expanded hyperlink showing subtopic information

Step 8

## Clues to Use

### Recovering lost presentation files

Sometimes while you are working on a presentation, PowerPoint may freeze, making it impossible to continue working on your presentation, or you may experience a power failure that causes your computer to shut down. If this type of interruption occurs, PowerPoint has a built-in recovery feature that allows you to open and save files that were open during the interruption. When you start PowerPoint again after an interruption, the Document Recovery task pane opens on the left side of your screen, displaying both original and recovered versions of the PowerPoint files that were open. If you're not sure which file to open (original or recovered), it's usually better to open the recovered file because it will have retained the latest information. You can, however, open and review all the versions of the file that was recovered and select the best one to save. Each file listed in the Document Recovery task pane has a list arrow with options that allow you to open the file, save the file, delete the file, or show repairs made to the file.

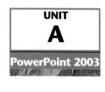

# Printing and Closing the File, and Exiting PowerPoint

You print your presentation when you have completed it or when you want to review your work. Reviewing hard copies of your presentation at different stages gives you an overall perspective of its content and look. When you are finished working on your presentation, even if it is not yet complete, you can close the presentation file and exit PowerPoint. ▰▰▰▰ You are done working on the presentation for now, so after you save the presentation, you print the slides and notes pages of the presentation so you can review them later; then you close the file and exit PowerPoint.

## STEPS

1. **Click File on the menu bar, then click Print**

   The Print dialog box opens. See Figure A-14. In this dialog box, you can specify which slide format you want to print (slides, handouts, notes pages, etc.), the slide range, the number of copies to print, as well as other print options. The default options for the available printer are selected in the dialog box.

2. **In the Print range section in the middle of the dialog box, click the Slides option button to select it, type 4 to print only the fourth slide, then click OK**

   The fourth slide prints. To save paper when you are reviewing your slides, it's a good idea to print in handout format, which lets you print up to nine slides per page.

3. **Click File on the menu bar, then click Print**

   The Print dialog box opens again. The options you choose in the Print dialog box remain there until you close the presentation.

4. **Click the All option button in the Print range section, click the Print what list arrow, click Handouts, click the Slides per page list arrow in the Handouts section, then click 6 if it is not already selected**

5. **Click the Color/grayscale list arrow, click Pure Black and White as shown in Figure A-15, then click OK**

   The presentation prints as handouts that you can give to your audience on three pages. The presentation prints without any gray tones. The pure black-and-white printing option can save printer toner.

6. **Click File on the menu bar, then click Print**

   The Print dialog box opens again.

7. **Click the Print what list arrow, click Outline View, then click OK**

   The outline for each slide in the presentation prints on three pages.

8. **Click File on the menu bar, then click Close**

   If you have made changes to your presentation, a Microsoft PowerPoint alert box opens asking you if you want to save changes you have made to the Marketing Campaign file.

9. **If necessary, click Yes to close the alert box**

10. **Click File on the menu bar, then click Exit**

    The presentation and the PowerPoint program close, and you return to the Windows desktop.

FIGURE A-14: Print dialog box

Your printer name
may be different

Slides option button

Click to select an
item to print

Color/grayscale
list arrow

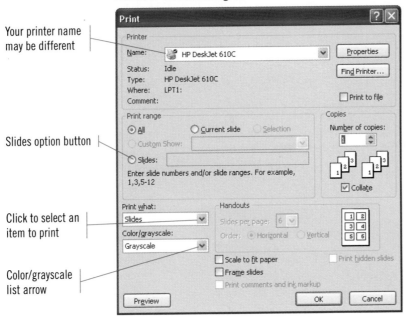

FIGURE A-15: Print dialog box with Handouts selected

Print what list arrow

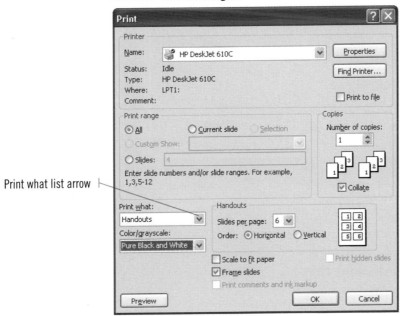

## Clues to Use

### Viewing your presentation in grayscale or black and white

Viewing your presentation in pure black and white or in grayscale (using shades of gray) is very useful when you are printing a presentation on a black-and-white printer and you want to make sure your text is readable. To see how your color presentation looks in grayscale or black and white, click the Color/Grayscale button 🔲 on the Standard toolbar, then click either Grayscale or Pure Black and White. The Grayscale View toolbar appears. You can use the

Grayscale View toolbar to select different settings to view your presentation. If you don't like the way an object looks in black and white or grayscale view, you can change its color. Right-click the object, point to Black and White Setting or Grayscale Setting (depending on which view you are in), and choose from the options on the submenu.

# Practice

## ▼ CONCEPTS REVIEW

**Label each element of the PowerPoint window shown in Figure A-16.**

FIGURE A-16

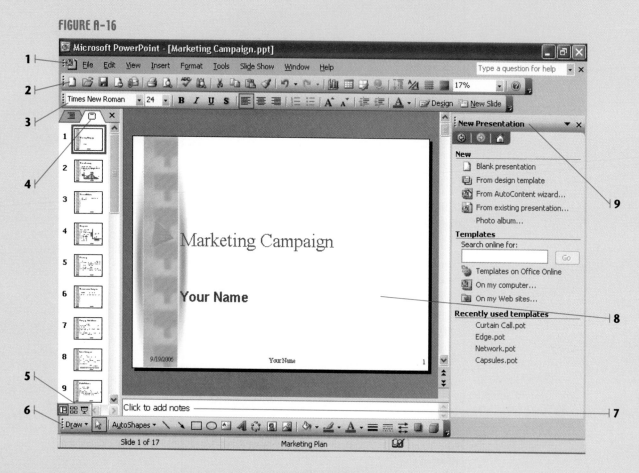

**Match each term with the statement that best describes it.**

10. Notes pane
11. Slide Sorter view
12. Task pane
13. Normal view
14. Slides tab

a. Displays hyperlinks of common commands
b. Displays the slides of your presentation as thumbnails in Normal view
c. A pane in Normal view that allows you to type notes that reference a slide's content
d. Displays the Outline and Slides tabs, as well as the slide and notes panes
e. A view that shows all your slides as thumbnails

## Select the best answer from the list of choices.

**15. All of the following are PowerPoint views, *except*:**
- **a.** Slide Sorter view
- **b.** Notes Page view
- **c.** Current Page view
- **d.** Normal view

**16. PowerPoint can help you create all of the following, *except*:**
- **a.** A Web presentation
- **b.** Outline pages
- **c.** An on-screen presentation
- **d.** A digital movie

**17. The buttons you use to switch between the PowerPoint views are called:**
- **a.** Screen buttons
- **b.** View buttons
- **c.** PowerPoint buttons
- **d.** Toolbar buttons

**18. The view that allows you to view your electronic slide show with each slide filling the entire screen is called:**
- **a.** Slide Sorter view
- **b.** Presentation view
- **c.** Slide Show view
- **d.** Electronic view

**19. How do you switch to Notes Page view?**
- **a.** Press [Shift] and click in the notes pane.
- **b.** Click the Notes Page View button.
- **c.** Click View on the menu bar, then click Notes Page.
- **d.** All of the above.

**20. How do you save changes to your presentation after you have saved it for the first time?**
- **a.** Click Save As on the File menu, select a filename from the list, then assign it a new name.
- **b.** Click the Save button on the Standard toolbar.
- **c.** Click Save As on the File menu, then click Save.
- **d.** Click Save As on the File menu, specify a new location and filename, then click Save.

**21. Which wizard helps you create and outline your presentation?**
- **a.** Presentation Wizard
- **b.** OrgContent Wizard
- **c.** AutoContent Wizard
- **d.** Topic Wizard

# ▼ SKILLS REVIEW

**1. Start PowerPoint and view the PowerPoint window.**

   **a.** Identify as many elements of the PowerPoint window as you can without referring to the unit material.

   **b.** Describe the purpose or function of each element.

   **c.** For any elements you cannot identify, refer to the unit.

**2. Use the AutoContent Wizard.**

   **a.** Start the AutoContent Wizard, then select a presentation category and type. (*Hint*: If you see a message saying you need to install the feature, insert your Office CD in the appropriate drive and click OK. If you are working in a networked computer lab, see your technical support person for assistance. If you are unable to load additional templates, click No as many times as necessary, then select another presentation type.)

   **b.** Select the output option of your choice.

   **c.** Enter an appropriate title for the opening slide, enter your name as the footer text, and complete the wizard to show the first slide of the presentation.

**3. View a presentation and run a slide show.**

   **a.** View each slide in the presentation to become familiar with its content.

   **b.** When you are finished, return to Slide 1.

   **c.** Click the Outline tab and review the presentation contents.

   **d.** Change to Notes Page view and see if the notes pages in the presentation contain text, then return to Normal view.

   **e.** Examine the presentation contents in Slide Sorter view.

   **f.** View all the slides of the presentation in Slide Show view, and end the slide show to return to Slide Sorter view.

**4. Save a presentation.**

   **a.** Change to Notes Page view.

   **b.** Open the Save As dialog box.

   **c.** Navigate to the drive and folder where your Data Files are stored.

   **d.** Name your presentation **Practice**.

   **e.** Click Tools on the menu bar, then click Save Options.

   **f.** Choose the option to embed the fonts in your presentation, as shown in Figure A-17, then click OK.

   **g.** Save your file.

   **h.** Go to a different view than the one you saved your presentation in.

   **i.** Save the changed presentation.

FIGURE A-17

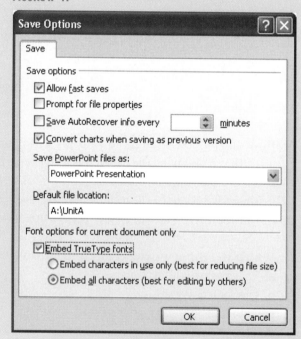

# ▼ SKILLS REVIEW (CONTINUED)

## 5. Get Help and Research Information.

a. Type **creating presentations** in the Type a question for help box, then press [Enter].

b. Click the down scroll arrow in the results list, then click the Create a presentation using a design template hyperlink.

c. Read the information, then click and read the Tip hyperlink.

d. Click the Help Window Close button.

e. Click the Other Task Panes list arrow, then click Research.

f. Type **PowerPoint presentations** in the Search for text box.

g. Click the Search for list arrow, then click All Research Sites.

h. Read the results that appear.

## 6. Print and close the file, and exit PowerPoint.

a. Print slides 2 and 3 as slides in grayscale. (*Hint*: In the Slides text box, type **2-3**.)

b. Print all the slides as handouts, 9 slides per page, in pure black and white.

c. Print the presentation outline.

d. Close the file, saving your changes.

e. Exit PowerPoint.

# ▼ INDEPENDENT CHALLENGE 1

You own a small photography business where most of your revenue comes from customized portraits for special occasions, such as weddings. In an effort to expand your business and appeal to more consumers, you decide to investigate various ways for you to display and send customer's personal photographs over the Internet. You have recently been using PowerPoint to create marketing presentations and you decide to learn more about PowerPoint's Photo Album feature using PowerPoint Help.

a. If PowerPoint is not already running, start it.

b. Use PowerPoint Help to find information on how to publish a photo album to the Web. (*Hint*: Type **photo album** in the Type a question for help box.)

c. Write down the steps you followed to get this information, then add your name to the document.

d. Print the Help window that shows the information you found. (*Hint*: Click the Print button at the top of the Help window.)

## Advanced Challenge Exercise

- Use the Research task pane to search for Web sites that relate to photo albums on the Web.
- Click a Web site hyperlink in the Research task pane results list to explore the Web page contents.
- Print the Home page of the Web site you visit.
- Close your Web browser program.

e. Exit PowerPoint.

# ▼ INDEPENDENT CHALLENGE 2

You are in charge of marketing for ArtWorks, Inc., a medium-size company that produces all types of art for corporations to enhance their work environment. The company has a regional sales area that includes areas throughout Western Europe. The president of ArtWorks asks you to plan and create the outline of the PowerPoint presentation he will use to convey a new Internet service that ArtWorks is developing.

    **a.** If necessary, start PowerPoint.

    **b.** Start the AutoContent Wizard. (*Hint*: If the task pane is not visible, click View on the menu bar, then click Task Pane.)

    **c.** On the Presentation type screen, choose the Sales/Marketing category, then choose Product/Services Overview from the list.

    **d.** Choose the Web presentation output, then assign the presentation an appropriate title, and include your name as the footer text.

    **e.** Scroll through the outline that the AutoContent Wizard produces. Does it contain the type of information you thought it would?

    **f.** Plan and take notes on how you would change and add to the sample text created by the wizard. What information do you need to promote ArtWorks to companies?

    **g.** Switch views. Run through the slide show at least once.

    **h.** Save your presentation with the name **ArtWorks Online** to the drive and folder where your Data Files are stored.

    **i.** Print your presentation as handouts (six slides per page).

    **j.** Close the presentation and exit PowerPoint.

# ▼ INDEPENDENT CHALLENGE 3

You have recently been promoted to sales manager at Turner Industries. Part of your job is to train sales representatives to go to potential customers and give presentations describing your company's products. Your boss wants you to find an appropriate PowerPoint presentation template that you can use for your next training presentation to recommend strategies to the sales representatives for closing sales. She wants a printout so she can evaluate it.

    **a.** If necessary, start PowerPoint.

    **b.** Start the AutoContent Wizard. (*Hint*: If the task pane is not visible, click View on the menu bar, then click Task Pane.)

    **c.** Examine the available AutoContent Wizards and select one that you could adapt for your presentation. (*Hint*: If you see a message saying you need to install additional templates, insert your Office CD in the appropriate drive and click OK. If you are working in a networked computer lab, see your technical support person for assistance. If you are unable to load additional templates, click No as many times as necessary, then select another presentation type.)

    **d.** Choose the On-screen presentation type, then enter an appropriate slide title and include your name as the footer text.

    **e.** Print the presentation as an outline, then print the first slide in pure black and white.

    **f.** Write a brief memo to your boss describing which wizard you think is most helpful, referring to specific slides in the outline to support your recommendation.

    **g.** Save the presentation as **Turner Training** to the drive and folder where your Data Files are stored.

    **h.** Close the presentation and exit PowerPoint.

# ▼ INDEPENDENT CHALLENGE 4

In this unit, you've learned about PowerPoint basics such as how to start PowerPoint, view the PowerPoint window, use the AutoContent Wizard, and run a slide show. There are many Web sites that provide information about how to use PowerPoint more effectively.

Use the Microsoft Web site to access information about the following topic:

- Presentation Tips

**a.** Connect to the Internet, then go to Microsoft's Web site at www.microsoft.com.

**b.** In the Search for text box, type **Dale Carnegie Training**, then press [Enter].

**c.** Locate the hyperlink that provides information on presentation tips from Dale Carnegie Training, then click the hyperlink. See Figure A-18.

**d.** Print and read the article, then write your name and course identification on the printed document.

### Advanced Challenge Exercise

- Create and save a document as **Presentation Tips** to the drive and folder where your Data Files are stored.
- Type your name and course identification at the top of the document.
- The Web article identifies a four-step process for delivering an effective presentation. Using the information in the Web article, identify each of these steps and the most important subpoint. Explain your answers.
- Save your final document, print it, close the document, then exit your word processing program.

**e.** Exit your Web browser program.

FIGURE A-18

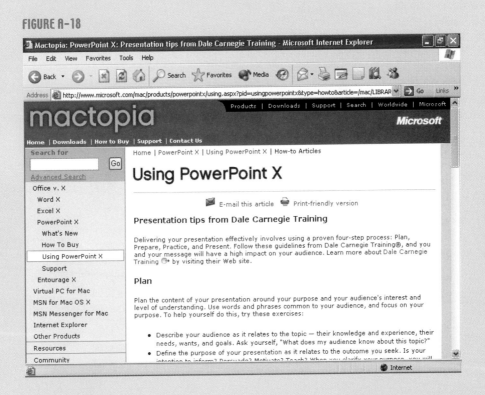

PowerPoint 2003

# ▼ VISUAL WORKSHOP

Create the presentation shown in Figure A-19 using the Project Post-Mortem AutoContent Wizard in the Projects category. Make sure you include your name as the footer. Save the presentation as **Triad** to the drive and folder where your Data Files are stored. Print the slides as handouts, six slides per page, in pure black and white.

FIGURE A-19

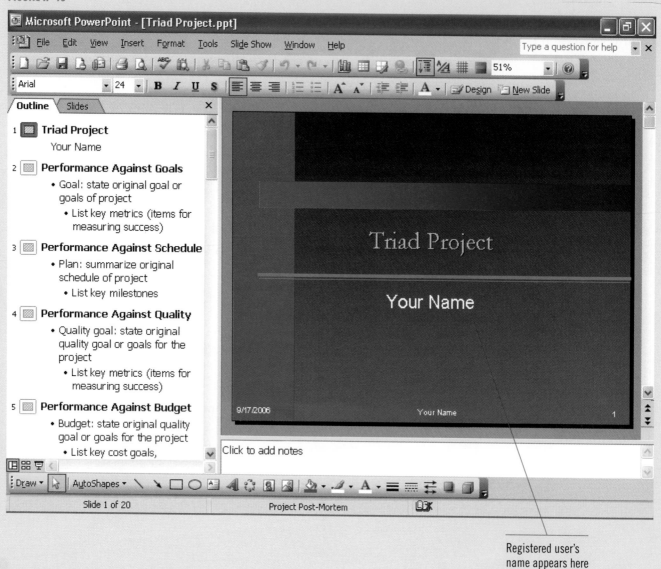

Registered user's name appears here

# Creating a Presentation

## OBJECTIVES

Plan an effective presentation

Enter slide text

Create a new slide

Enter text in the Outline tab

Add slide headers and footers

Choose a look for a presentation

Check spelling in a presentation

Evaluate a presentation

If you have a SAM user profile, you may have access to hands-on instruction, practice, and assessment of the skills covered in this unit. Log in to your SAM account and go to your assignments page to see what your instructor has assigned.

Now that you are familiar with PowerPoint basics, you are ready to plan and create your own presentation. To do this, you first enter and edit the presentation text, and then you can focus on the design and look of the presentation. PowerPoint helps you accomplish these tasks. You can start with the AutoContent Wizard and then enhance the look of your presentation by selecting a design from a collection of professionally prepared slide designs, called **design templates**. In this unit, you create a presentation using a PowerPoint design template. Maria Abbott, general sales manager at MediaLoft, asks you to prepare a marketing presentation on a new service that MediaLoft is planning to introduce. You begin by planning your presentation.

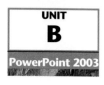

# Planning an Effective Presentation

Before you create a presentation using PowerPoint, you need to plan and outline the message you want to communicate and consider how you want the presentation to look. When preparing the outline, you need to keep in mind where you are giving the presentation and who your audience is. It is also important to know what equipment you might need, such as a sound system, computer, or projector. Use the planning guidelines below to help plan an effective presentation. Figure B-1 illustrates a well thought-out presentation outline.

## In planning a presentation, it is important to:

- **Determine the purpose of the presentation**

  When you have a well-defined purpose, developing an outline for your presentation is much easier. You need to present a marketing plan for a new Internet service that MediaLoft is planning to launch later in the year.

- **Determine the message you want to communicate, then give the presentation a meaningful title and outline your message**

  If possible, take time to adequately develop an outline of your presentation content before creating the slides. Start your presentation by defining the new service, describing the competition, and stating the product positioning. See Figure B-1.

- **Determine the audience and the delivery location**

  The presentation audience and delivery location can greatly affect the type of presentation you create. For example, if you had to deliver a presentation to your staff in a small, dimly lit conference room, you may create a very simple presentation with a bright color scheme; however, if you had to deliver a sales presentation to a client in a formal conference room with many windows, you may need to create a very professional-looking presentation with a darker color scheme. You will deliver this presentation in a large conference room to MediaLoft's marketing management team.

- **Determine the type of output—black-and-white or color overhead transparencies, on-screen slide show, or an online broadcast—that best conveys your message, given time constraints and computer hardware availability**

  Because you are speaking in a large conference room to a large group and have access to a computer and projection equipment, you decide that an on-screen slide show is the best output choice for your presentation.

- **Determine a look for your presentation that will help communicate your message**

  You can choose one of the professionally designed templates that come with PowerPoint, modify one of these templates, or create one of your own. You want a simple and artistic template to convey the marketing plan.

- **Determine what additional materials will be useful in the presentation**

  You need to prepare not only the slides themselves but also supplementary materials, including speaker notes and handouts for the audience. You use speaker notes to help remember a few key details, and you pass out handouts for the audience to use as a reference.

FIGURE B-1: Outline of the presentation content

1. eMedia
    - Proposed Marketing Plan
    - Your Name
    - August 12, 2006
    - Director of Internet Services
2. Product Definition
    - Internet media provider
        - Music and video
        - Articles and trade papers
        - Historical papers archive
    - On-demand publishing
        - Articles, books, research papers, games, and more...
3. Competition
    - Bookstores
    - Internet services
    - Media services
    - Ratings
4. Product Positioning
    - Licensed media download service provider
    - Interactive service provider
    - Publishing service provider

PowerPoint 2003

## Clues to Use

### Using templates from the Web

When you create a presentation, you have the option of using one of the design templates supplied with PowerPoint, or you can use a template from another source, such as a Web server or the Template Gallery on the Microsoft Office Web site. To create a presentation using a template from a Web server, start PowerPoint, open the New Presentation task pane, then click the On my Web sites hyperlink under Templates. The New from Templates on my Web Sites dialog box opens. Locate and open the template you want to use, then save it with a new name. To use a template from the Microsoft Office Online Web site, open the New Presentation task pane, then click the Templates on Office Online hyperlink. Your Web browser opens to the Microsoft Office Online Templates Web site. Locate the PowerPoint template you want to use, then click the Download Now button to open and save the template in PowerPoint. The first time you use the Templates Web site, you must install the Microsoft Office Template and MediaControl and accept the license agreement.

# Entering Slide Text

Each time you start PowerPoint, a new presentation with a blank title slide appears in Normal view. The title slide has two **text placeholders**—boxes with dashed-line borders—where you enter text. The top text placeholder on the title slide is the **title placeholder**, labeled "Click to add title". The bottom text placeholder on the title slide is the **Subtitle text placeholder**, labeled "Click to add subtitle". To enter text in a placeholder, simply click the placeholder and then type your text. After you enter text in a placeholder, the placeholder becomes a text object. An **object** is any item on a slide that can be manipulated. Objects are the building blocks that make up a presentation slide. ▓▓▓▓ Begin working on your presentation by starting PowerPoint and entering text on the title slide.

**STEPS**

1. **Start PowerPoint**

   A new presentation appears displaying a blank title slide in Normal view.

2. **Move the pointer over the title placeholder labeled "Click to add title" in the Slide pane**

   The pointer changes to I when you move the pointer over the placeholder. In PowerPoint, the pointer often changes shape, depending on the task you are trying to accomplish.

3. **Click the title placeholder in the Slide pane**

   The **insertion point**, a blinking vertical line, indicates where your text appears when you type in the title placeholder. A **selection box**, the slanted line border, appears around the title placeholder, indicating that it is selected and ready to accept text. See Figure B-2.

   **TROUBLE**

   If you press a wrong key, press [Backspace] to erase the character.

4. **Type eMedia**

   PowerPoint center-aligns the title text within the title placeholder, which is now a text object. Notice that text appears on the slide thumbnail in the slides tab.

5. **Click the subtitle text placeholder in the Slide pane**

   A wavy red line may appear under the word "eMedia" in the title text object indicating that the automatic spellchecking feature in PowerPoint is active. If it doesn't appear on your screen, it may mean that the automatic spellchecking feature is turned off.

6. **Type Proposed Marketing Plan, then press [Enter]**

   The insertion point moves to the next line in the Subtitle text object.

7. **Type Your Name, press [Enter], type August 12, 2006, press [Enter], then type Director of Internet Services**

   Notice that the AutoFit Options button ▣ appears near the text object. The AutoFit Options button on your screen indicates that PowerPoint has automatically decreased the size of all the text in the text object to fit in the text object.

8. **Click the Autofit Options button ▣, then click Stop Fitting Text to This Placeholder on the shortcut menu**

   The text in the Subtitle text box changes back to its original size.

   **TROUBLE**

   If the insertion point is blinking in a blank line after completing this step, press [Backspace] one more time.

9. **Position I to the right of 2006, drag to select the entire line of text, press [Backspace], then click outside the main text object in a blank area of the slide**

   The text and the line the text was on are deleted and the Autofit Options button closes, as shown in Figure B-3. Clicking a blank area of the slide deselects all selected objects on the slide.

10. **Click the Save button ▣ on the Standard toolbar, then save your presentation as eMediaB to the drive and folder where your Data Files are stored**

**FIGURE B-2:** Slide with selected title text placeholder

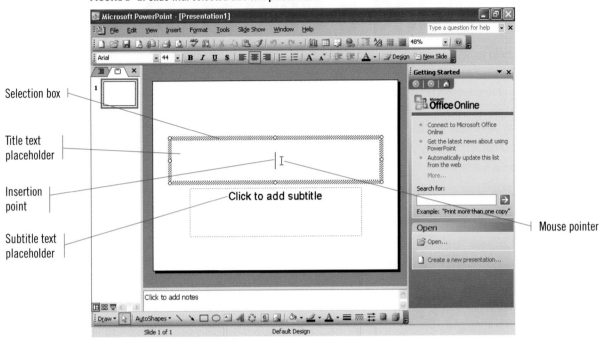

Selection box

Title text placeholder

Insertion point

Subtitle text placeholder

Mouse pointer

**FIGURE B-3:** Title slide with text

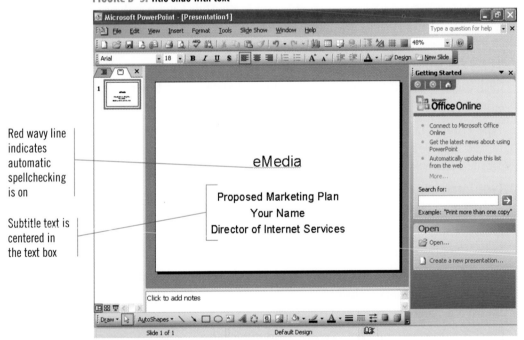

Red wavy line indicates automatic spellchecking is on

Subtitle text is centered in the text box

## Clues to Use

### Using Speech Recognition

Speech recognition technology lets you enter text and issue commands in PowerPoint by talking into a standard microphone connected to your computer. It is an Office-wide program that you must install and set up before you can use it. To set up Speech Recognition, start Microsoft Word, click Tools on the menu bar, then click Speech. You might be prompted to install the Speech Recognition files using the Office CD. Once you have installed the Speech Recognition files, the Speech Recognition component is available in all Office programs, including PowerPoint. To begin

using Speech Recognition, you first need to train your computer to understand how you speak by using a Training Wizard. A Training Wizard is a series of paragraphs that you read into your computer's microphone. These training sessions teach the Speech module to recognize your voice. They also teach you the speed and level of clarity with which you need to speak so that the program can understand you. Training sessions improve the performance of the Speech Recognition module. If you don't use the training sessions, the Speech Recognition module may be inaccurate.

# Creating a New Slide

To help you create a new slide easily, PowerPoint offers 27 predesigned slide layouts. A **slide layout** determines how all of the elements on a slide are arranged. Slide layouts include a variety of placeholder arrangements for different objects, including text, clip art, tables, charts, diagrams, and media clips. Layouts are organized by type in the following categories: text layouts, content layouts, text and content layouts, and other layouts. You have already used the Title Slide layout in the previous lesson. Table B-1 describes some of the placeholders you'll find in PowerPoint's slide layouts. To continue developing the presentation, you create a slide that defines the new service MediaLoft is developing.

**STEPS**

**QUICK TIP**

You can also insert a new slide from the Slide Layout task pane: point to the slide layout you want, click the slide layout list arrow, then click Insert New Slide.

1. **Click the New Slide button 📄 on the Formatting toolbar**

   A new blank slide (now the current slide) appears as the second slide in your presentation and the Slide Layout task pane opens, as shown in Figure B-4. The new slide in the Slide pane contains a title placeholder and a **body text placeholder** for a bulleted list. Notice that the status bar indicates Slide 2 of 2 and that the Slides tab now contains two slide thumbnails. The Slide Layout task pane identifies the different PowerPoint slide layouts that you can use in your presentation. A dark border appears around the Title and Text slide layout identifying it as the currently applied layout for the slide. You can easily change the current slide's layout by clicking a slide layout icon in the Slide Layout task pane.

2. **Point to the Title and 2-Column Text layout in the Slide Layout task pane**

   When you place your pointer over a slide layout icon, a selection list arrow appears. You can click the list arrow to choose options for applying the layout. After a brief moment, a ScreenTip also appears that identifies the slide layout by name.

3. **Click the Title and 2-Column Text layout in the Slide Layout task pane**

   A slide layout with two text placeholders replaces the Title and Text slide layout for the current slide.

**TROUBLE**

When AutoCorrect is active, if you mistype a common word, PowerPoint automatically corrects it when you press [Spacebar] or [Enter]. You know PowerPoint has automatically corrected a word when you point to a word and a small rectangle appears under the word. To see a list of common typing errors that PowerPoint corrects automatically, click Tools on the menu bar, then click AutoCorrect Options.

4. **Type Product Definition, then click the left body text placeholder in the Slide pane**

   The text you type appears in the title placeholder, and the insertion point appears next to a bullet in the left body text placeholder.

5. **Type Internet media provider, then press [Enter]**

   A new first-level bullet automatically appears when you press [Enter].

6. **Press [Tab]**

   The new first-level bullet indents and becomes a second-level bullet.

7. **Type Music and video, press [Enter], type Articles and trade papers, press [Enter], then type Historical papers archive**

   The left text object now has four bulleted points.

8. **Press [Ctrl][Enter], then type On-demand publishing**

   Pressing [Ctrl][Enter] moves the insertion point to the next text placeholder on the slide. Because this is a two-column layout, the insertion point moves to the other body text placeholder on the slide.

9. **Press [Enter], click the Increase Indent button ▤ on the Formatting toolbar, enter the four second-level bulleted items shown in Figure B-5, click in a blank area of the slide, then click the Save button 💾 on the Standard toolbar**

   The Increase Indent button indents the first-level bullet, which changes it to a second-level bullet. Clicking the Save button saves all of the changes to the file. Compare your screen with Figure B-5.

**FIGURE B-4:** New blank slide in Normal view

New slide thumbnail added to Slides tab

Body text placeholder

Total number of slides

Current slide number

New Slide button

Slide Layout task pane may appear differently on your screen

Title and 2-column Text layout

Current slide layout

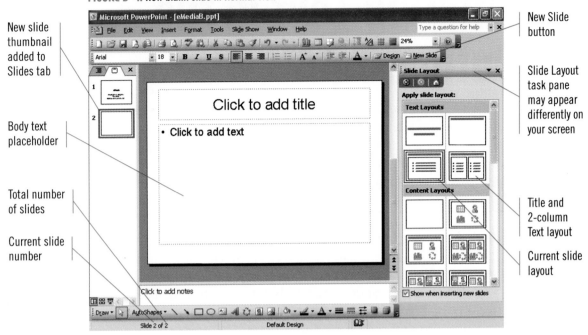

**FIGURE B-5:** New slide with Title and 2-Column Text slide layout

Save button

First-level bullet

Second-level bullet

Two text objects based on the slide layout

Type this text to complete Step 9

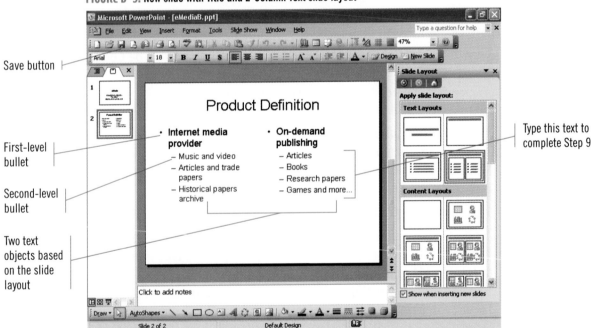

**TABLE B-1:** Slide Layout placeholders

| placeholder | symbol | description |
|---|---|---|
| Bulleted List | | Inserts a short list of related points |
| Clip Art | | Inserts a picture from the Clip Organizer |
| Chart | | Inserts a chart created with Microsoft Graph |
| Diagram or Organization Chart | | Inserts a diagram or organizational chart |
| Table | | Inserts a table |
| Media Clip | | Inserts a music, sound, or video clip |
| Content | | Inserts objects such as a table, a chart, clip art, a picture, a diagram or organizational chart, or a media clip |

# Entering Text in the Outline Tab

You can enter presentation text by typing directly on the slide, as you've learned already, or, if you'd rather focus on the presentation text without worrying about the layout, you can enter it in the Outline tab. As in a regular outline, the headings, or titles, appear first; beneath the titles, the subpoints, or body text, appear. Body text appears as one or more lines of bulleted text indented under a title. ▓▓▓▓ You switch to the Outline tab to enter body text for two more slides.

## STEPS

**QUICK TIP**

The commands on the Outlining tool-bar can be helpful when working in the Outline tab. To open the Outlining tool-bar, click View on the menu bar, point to Toolbars, then click Outlining.

1. **Click the Outline tab to the left of the Slide pane**

   The Outline tab enlarges to display the text that is on your slides. The slide icon for Slide 2 is highlighted, indicating that it's selected. Notice the numbers 1 and 2 that appear to the left of each of the first-level bullets for Slide 2, indicating that there are two body text objects on the slide.

2. **Point to the Title and Text layout in the Slide Layout task pane, click the list arrow, then click Insert New Slide**

   A new slide, Slide 3, with the Title and Text layout appears as the current slide below Slide 2. A selected slide icon ▢ appears next to the slide number in the Outline tab when you add a new slide. See Figure B-6. Text that you enter next to a slide icon becomes the title for that slide.

3. **Click to the right of the Slide 3 slide icon in the Outline tab, type Competition, press [Enter], then press [Tab]**

   A new slide is inserted when you press [Enter], but because you want to enter body text for the slide you just created, you press Tab, which indents this line to make it part of Slide 3.

4. **Type Bookstoes, press [Enter], type E-sites, press [Enter], type Media services, press [Enter], type Ratings, then press [Enter]**

   Make sure you typed "Bookstoes" without the "r" as specified in the step.

5. **Press [Shift][Tab]**

   The bullet that was created when you pressed [Enter] changes to a new slide icon.

6. **Type Product Positioning, press [Ctrl][Enter], type Licensed media download provider, press [Enter], type Publishing service provider, press [Enter], type Interactive service provider, then press [Ctrl][Enter]**

   Pressing [Ctrl][Enter] while the cursor is in the title text object moves the cursor into the body text object. Pressing [Ctrl][Enter] while the cursor is in the body text object creates a new slide with the same layout as the previous slide. Two of the bulleted points you just typed for Slide 4 are out of order, and you don't need the new Slide 5 you just created.

**QUICK TIP**

If you click the Undo button list arrow, you can select which actions you want to undo.

7. **Click the Undo button 🔄 on the Standard toolbar**

   Clicking the Undo button undoes the previous action. Slide 5 is deleted and the insertion point moves back up to the last bullet in Slide 4.

8. **Position the pointer to the left of the last bullet in Slide 4 in the Outline tab**

   The pointer changes to ⊕.

**TROUBLE**

If your screen does not match Figure B-7, drag the text to the correct location.

9. **Drag the mouse up until the pointer changes to ↕ and a horizontal indicator line appears above the second bullet point in Slide 4, then release the mouse button**

   The third bullet point moves up one line in the outline and trades places with the second bullet point, as shown in Figure B-7.

10. **Click the Slides tab, click the Slide 2 thumbnail in the Slides tab, then save your work**

    Slide 2 of 4 should appear in the status bar.

**FIGURE B-6:** Normal view with Outline tab open

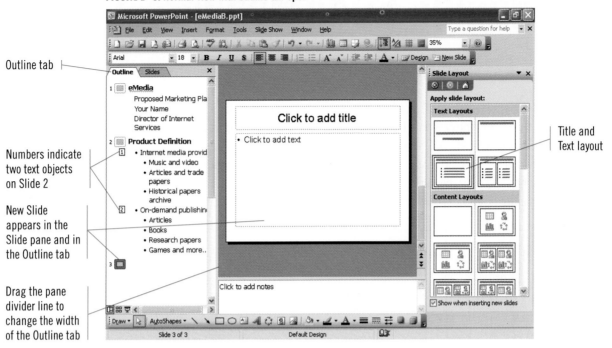

Outline tab

Numbers indicate two text objects on Slide 2

New Slide appears in the Slide pane and in the Outline tab

Drag the pane divider line to change the width of the Outline tab

Title and Text layout

**FIGURE B-7:** Bulleted item moved up in the Outline tab

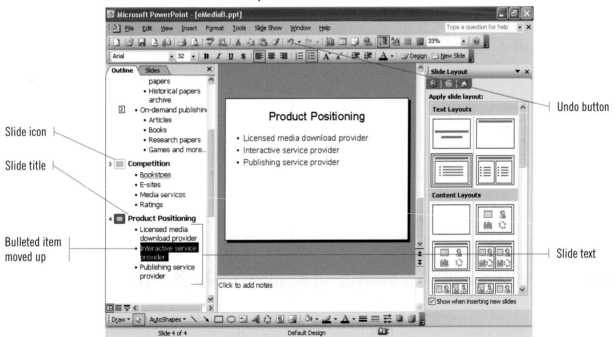

Slide icon

Slide title

Bulleted item moved up

Undo button

Slide text

## Clues to Use

### What do I do if I see a lightbulb on a slide?

If you are showing the Office Assistant, you may see a yellow lightbulb in your presentation window. The lightbulb is part of the PowerPoint Help system and it can mean several things. First, the Office Assistant might have a suggestion for an appropriate piece of clip art for that slide. Second, the Office Assistant might have a helpful tip based on the task you are performing. This is known as a context-sensitive tip. Third, the Office Assistant might have detected a style, such as a word in the slide title that should be capitalized, which is inconsistent with preset style guidelines. When you see a lightbulb, you can click it, read the dialog balloon, and click the option you prefer, or you can ignore it. If the Office Assistant is hidden or turned off, the lightbulb does not appear.

# Adding Slide Headers and Footers

Header and footer text, such as your company or product name, the slide number, and the date, can give your slides a professional look and make it easier for your audience to follow your presentation. On slides, you can add text only to the footer; however, notes or handouts can include both header and footer text. Footer information that you apply to the slides of your presentation is visible in the PowerPoint views and when you print the slides. Notes and handouts header and footer text is visible when you print notes pages, handouts, and the outline. ▰▰▰▰ You add footer text to the slides of your presentation.

## STEPS

1. **Click View on the menu bar, then click Header and Footer**

   The Header and Footer dialog box opens, as shown in Figure B-8. The Header and Footer dialog box has two tabs: a Slide tab and a Notes and Handouts tab. The Slide tab is selected. There are three types of footer text, Date and time, Slide number, and Footer. The Date and time and the Footer check boxes are selected by default. The rectangles at the bottom of the Preview box identify the default position and status of the three types of footer text on the slides. Two of the rectangles at the bottom of the Preview box have dark borders.

2. **Click the Date and time check box to deselect it**

   The date and time suboptions are no longer available and the far-left rectangle at the bottom of the Preview box has a light border. The middle rectangle identifies where the Footer text—the only check box still selected—will appear on the slide. The rectangle on the right shows where the slide number will appear if you select that check box.

3. **Click the Date and time check box, then click the Update automatically option button**

   Now every time you view the slide show or print the slides in this presentation, the current date appears in the footer.

4. **Click the Update automatically list arrow, then click the fourth option in the list**

   The date format changes to display the Month spelled out, the date number, and four-digit year.

5. **Click the Slide number check box, click in the Footer text box, then type Your Name**

   The Preview box now shows that all three footer placeholders are selected.

6. **Click the Don't show on title slide check box**

   Selecting this check box prevents the footer information you entered in the Header and Footer dialog box from appearing on the title slide. Compare your screen to Figure B-9.

7. **Click Apply to All**

   The dialog box closes and the footer information is applied to all of the slides in your presentation except the title slide. You can click the Apply button to apply footer information to just one slide in the presentation if you want.

8. **Click the Slide 1 thumbnail in the Slides tab, click View on the menu bar, then click Header and Footer**

   The Header and Footer dialog box opens, displaying all of the options that you specified for the presentation. You want to show your company slogan in the footer on the title slide.

9. **Click the Date and time check box, the Slide number check box, and the Don't show on title slide check box to deselect them, then select the text in the Footer text box**

10. **Type "All Media...All the Time", click Apply, then save your work**

    Only the text in the Footer text box appears on the title slide. Clicking Apply applies the footer information to just the current slide.

FIGURE B-8: Header and Footer dialog box

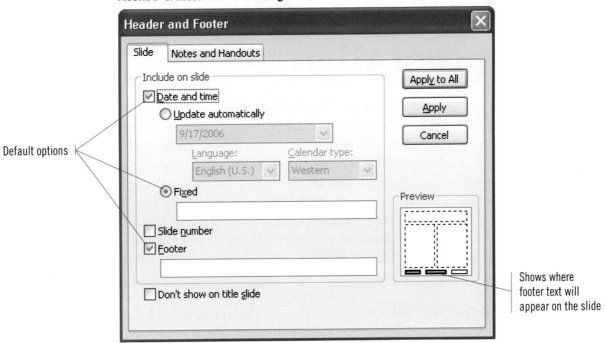

Default options

Shows where footer text will appear on the slide

FIGURE B-9: Completed Header and Footer dialog box

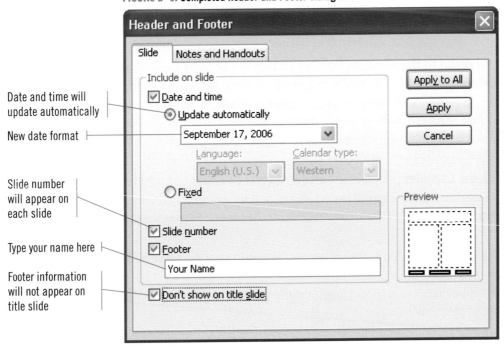

Date and time will update automatically

New date format

Slide number will appear on each slide

Type your name here

Footer information will not appear on title slide

## Clues to Use

### Entering and printing notes

You can add notes to your slides when there are certain facts you want to remember during a presentation or when there is information you want to hand out to your audience. Notes do not appear on the slides when you run a slide show. Use the Notes pane in Normal view or Notes Page view to enter notes for your slides. To enter text notes on a slide, click in the Notes pane, then type. If you want to insert graphics as notes, you must use Notes Page view. To open

Notes Page view, click View on the menu bar, then click Notes Page. You can print your notes by clicking the Print what list arrow and then clicking Notes Pages in the Print dialog box. The notes page can be a good handout to give your audience to use during the presentation and then after as a reminder. If you don't enter any notes in the Notes pane, and print the notes pages, the slides print as thumbnails with blank lines to the right of the thumbnails to handwrite notes.

# Choosing a Look for a Presentation

To help you design your presentation, PowerPoint provides a number of design templates so you can have professional help creating the right look for your presentation. A **design template** has borders, colors, text attributes, and other elements arranged to create a specific look. You can apply a design template to one or all the slides in your presentation. In most cases, you would apply one template to an entire presentation; you can, however, apply multiple templates to the same presentation, or a different template on each slide. You can use a design template as is, or you can modify any element to suit your needs. Unless you have training in graphic design, it is often easier and faster to use or modify one of the templates supplied with PowerPoint, rather than design your presentation from scratch. No matter how you create your presentation, you can save it as a template for future use. You decide to use an existing PowerPoint template.

## STEPS

1. **Click the Other Task Panes list arrow ▼ in the task pane title bar, then click Slide Design**

   The Slide Design task pane appears, similarly to the one shown in Figure B-10. This task pane is split into sections: the hyperlinks that open sub task panes are at the top of the pane; the Used in This Presentation section, which identifies the templates currently applied to the presentation (in this case, the Default Design template); the Recently Used section, which identifies up to four templates you have applied recently (this section does not appear on your screen if you have not used any other templates); and the Available For Use section, which lists all of the standard PowerPoint design templates that you can apply to a presentation.

2. **Scroll down to the Available For Use section of the Slide Design task pane, then place your pointer over the Capsules template (tenth row, second column)**

   A ScreenTip identifies the template, and a selection list arrow appears next to the Capsules template icon. The list arrow provides options for you to choose from when applying design templates. To determine how a design template looks on your presentation, you need to apply it. You can apply as many templates as you want until you find one that you like.

3. **Click the Capsules template list arrow, then click Apply to All Slides**

   The Capsules template is applied to all the slides. Notice the new slide background color, the new graphic elements, new fonts, and the new slide text color. You decide that this template doesn't work well with the presentation content.

4. **Click the Network template list arrow (eleventh row, first column), then click Apply to Selected Slides**

   The Network template is applied to just the title slide of the presentation. This design template doesn't fit with the presentation content either.

5. **Click the Edge template list arrow (eleventh row, second column), then click Apply to All Slides**

   This simple design template looks good with the presentation content and fits the MediaLoft company image.

6. **Click the Next Slide button ▼ three times**

   Preview all the slides in the presentation to see how they look.

7. **Click the Previous Slide button ▲ two times to return to Slide 2**

   Compare your screen to Figure B-11.

8. **Save your changes**

FIGURE B-10: Normal view with Slide Design task pane open

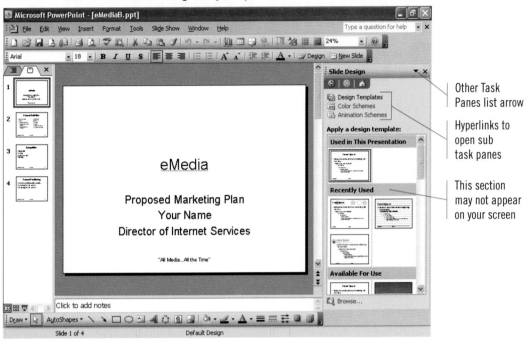

Other Task Panes list arrow

Hyperlinks to open sub task panes

This section may not appear on your screen

FIGURE B-11: Presentation with Edge template design applied

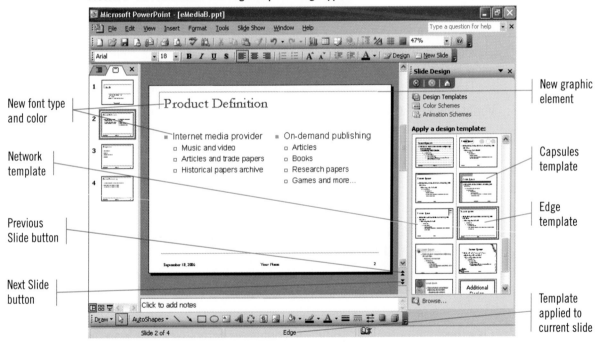

New font type and color

Network template

Previous Slide button

Next Slide button

New graphic element

Capsules template

Edge template

Template applied to current slide

## Clues to Use

### Using design templates

You are not limited to using the templates PowerPoint provides; you can also modify a PowerPoint template or even create your own. For example, you might want to use your company's color as a slide background or incorporate your company's logo on every slide. If you modify an existing template, you can keep, change, or delete any color, graphic, or font. To create a new template, click Blank Presentation on the New Presentation task pane. Add the design elements to the slide to create the look you want for the presentation.

Open the Save As dialog box, click the Save as type list arrow, choose Design Template, name your template, then click Save. PowerPoint automatically adds the file extension .pot to the filename, saves the template to the Templates folder, and adds it to the Slide Design task pane so that you can use your customized template as a basis for all future presentations. To apply a template that you created to an existing presentation, open the presentation, then choose the template in the Slide Design task pane.

# Checking Spelling in a Presentation

As your work nears completion, you need to review and proofread your presentation thoroughly for errors. You can use the spellchecking feature in PowerPoint to check for and correct spelling errors. This feature compares the spelling of all the words in your presentation against the words contained in its electronic dictionary. You still must proofread your presentation for punctuation, grammar, and word-usage errors because the spellchecker recognizes only misspelled words, not misused words. For example, the spellchecker would not identify "The test" as an error, even if you had intended to type "The best." ▓▓▓▓ You're finished adding and changing text in the presentation, so you can now check the spelling in the presentation.

## STEPS

**TROUBLE**
If your spellchecker doesn't find the word "eMedia," then a previous user may have accidentally added it to the custom dictionary. Skip Steps 1 and 2 and continue with the lesson.

1. **Click the Slide 1 thumbnail in the Slides tab, then click the Spelling button 🗹 on the Standard toolbar**

   PowerPoint begins to check the spelling in your entire presentation. When PowerPoint finds a misspelled word or a word it doesn't recognize, the Spelling dialog box opens, as shown in Figure B-12. For an explanation of the commands available in the Spelling dialog box, see Table B-2. In this case, PowerPoint does not recognize "eMedia" on Slide 1. It suggests that you replace it with the word "media". You want the word to remain as you typed it.

2. **Click Ignore All**

   Clicking Ignore All tells the spellchecker not to stop at and question any more occurrences of this word in this presentation. The next word the spellchecker identifies as an error is the word "Bookstoes" in the body text object on Slide 3. In the Suggestions list box, the spellchecker suggests "Bookstores."

**QUICK TIP**
The spellchecker does not check the text in inserted pictures or objects.

3. **Verify that Bookstores is selected in the Suggestions list box, then click Change**

   If PowerPoint finds any other words it does not recognize, either change them or ignore them. When the spellchecker finishes checking your presentation, the Spelling dialog box closes, and an alert box opens with a message that the spelling check is complete.

4. **Click OK**

   The alert box closes. You are satisfied with the presentation so far and you decide to print it.

**TROUBLE**
If your preview window does not show the slide in color it is because you have selected a black and white printer.

5. **Click the Print Preview button 🔍 on the Standard toolbar**

   The Print Preview window opens, displaying the presentation's title slide as shown in Figure B-13.

6. **Make sure Slides is selected in the Print What list box, click the Options list arrow on the Print Preview toolbar, then click Frame Slides**

   The slides of your presentation print with a frame around each page.

7. **Click the Print button 🖨 Print... on the Print Preview toolbar, click OK in the Print dialog box, click the Close Preview button Close on the Print Preview toolbar, then save your presentation**

---

### Clues to Use

#### Checking spelling as you type

PowerPoint checks your spelling as you type. If you type a word that is not in the electronic dictionary, a wavy red line appears under it. To correct an error, right-click the misspelled word, then review the suggestions, which appear in the shortcut menu. You can select a suggestion, add the word you typed to your custom dictionary, or ignore it.

To turn off automatic spellchecking, click Tools on the menu bar, then click Options to open the Options dialog box. Click the Spelling and Style tab, and in the Spelling section, click the Check spelling as you type check box to deselect it. To temporarily hide the wavy red lines, click the Hide all spelling errors check box to select it.

FIGURE B-12: Spelling dialog box

Unrecognized word

Selected word from
Suggestions list

Alternate spellings

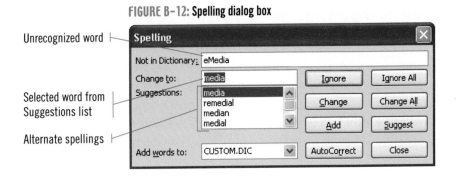

FIGURE B-13: Print Preview window

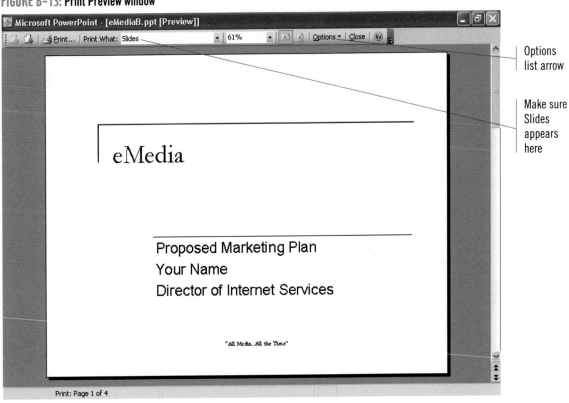

Options
list arrow

Make sure
Slides
appears
here

TABLE B-2: Spelling dialog box commands

| command | description |
| --- | --- |
| Ignore/Ignore All | Continues spellchecking without making any changes to the identified word (or all occurrences of the identified word) |
| Change/Change All | Changes the identified word (or all occurrences) to the suggested word |
| Add | Adds the identified word to your custom dictionary; spellchecker will not flag it again |
| Suggest | Suggests an alternative spelling for the identified word |
| AutoCorrect | Adds the suggested word as an AutoCorrect entry for the highlighted word |
| Add words to | Lets you choose a custom dictionary where you store words you often use but that are not part of the PowerPoint dictionary |

PowerPoint 2003

# Evaluating a Presentation

As you create a presentation, keep in mind that good design involves preparation. An effective presentation is both focused and visually appealing—easy for the speaker to present and easy for the audience to understand. The visual elements (colors, graphics, and text) can strongly influence the audience's attention and interest and can determine the success of your presentation. See Table B-3 for general information on the impact a visual presentation has on an audience. You take the time to evaluate your presentation's effectiveness.

### STEPS

1. **Click the Slide Show button [icon], then press [Enter] to move through the slide show**

2. **When you are finished viewing the slide show, click the Slide Sorter View button [icon]**
   You decide that Slide 4 should come before Slide 3.

3. **Drag Slide 4 between Slides 2 and 3, then release the mouse button**
   The thin black line that moved with the pointer indicates the slide's new position. The final presentation is shown in Slide Sorter view. Compare your screen to Figure B-14.

4. **When you are finished evaluating your presentation according to the guidelines below, save your changes, then close the presentation and exit PowerPoint**
   Figure B-15 shows a poorly designed slide. Contrast this slide with your eMedia presentation as you review the following guidelines.

### DETAILS

### When evaluating a presentation, it is important to:

- **Keep your message focused**
  Don't put everything you plan to say on your presentation slides. Keep the audience anticipating further explanations to the key points shown in the presentation.

- **Keep your text concise**
  Limit each slide to six words per line and six lines per slide. Use lists and symbols to help prioritize your points visually. Your presentation text provides only the highlights; use notes to give more detailed information. Your presentation focuses attention on the key issues and you supplement the information with further explanation and details during your presentation.

- **Keep the design simple, easy to read, and appropriate for the content**
  A design template makes the presentation consistent. If you design your own layout, keep it simple and use design elements sparingly. Use similar design elements consistently throughout the presentation; otherwise, your audience may get confused. You used a simple design template; the horizontal lines give the presentation a somewhat artistic look, which is appropriate for a casual professional presentation.

- **Choose attractive colors that make the slide easy to read**
  Use contrasting colors for slide background and text to make the text readable. If you are giving an on-screen presentation, you can use almost any combination of colors that look good together.

- **Choose fonts and styles that are easy to read and emphasize important text**
  As a general rule, use no more than two fonts in a presentation and vary the font size, using nothing smaller than 24 points. Use bold and italic attributes selectively.

- **Use visuals to help communicate the message of your presentation**
  Commonly used visuals include clip art, photographs, charts, worksheets, tables, and movies. Whenever possible, replace text with a visual, but be careful not to overcrowd your slides. White space on your slides is OK!

FIGURE B-14: The final presentation in Slide Sorter view

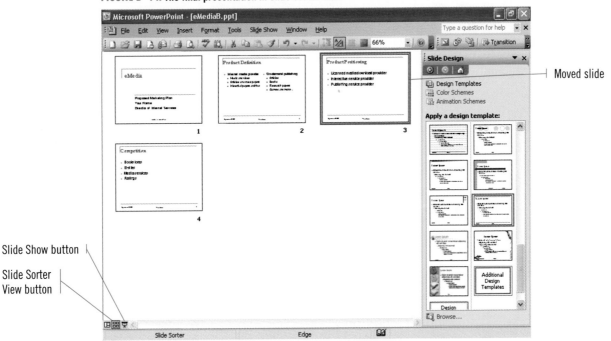

Moved slide

Slide Show button

Slide Sorter View button

FIGURE B-15: A poorly designed slide in Normal view

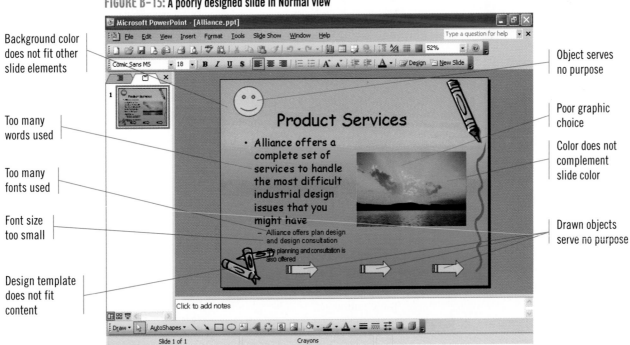

Background color does not fit other slide elements

Too many words used

Too many fonts used

Font size too small

Design template does not fit content

Object serves no purpose

Poor graphic choice

Color does not complement slide color

Drawn objects serve no purpose

TABLE B-3: Audience impact from a visual presentation

| impact | description |
| --- | --- |
| Visual reception | Most people receive up to 75% of all environmental stimuli through the human sense of sight |
| Learning | Up to 90% of what an audience learns comes from visual and audio messages |
| Retention | Combining visual messages with verbal messages can increase memory retention by as much as 30% |
| Presentation goals | You are twice as likely to achieve your communication objectives using a visual presentation |
| Meeting length | You are likely to decrease the average meeting length by 25% when you use visual presentation |

*Source: Presenters Online, www.presentersonline.com*

# Practice

## ▼ CONCEPTS REVIEW

**Label each element of the PowerPoint window shown in Figure B-16.**

FIGURE B-16

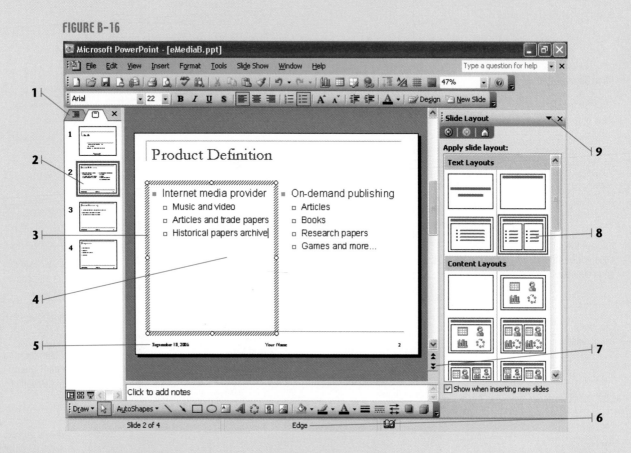

**Match each term with the statement that best describes it.**

10. Text placeholder
11. Slide layout
12. Selection box
13. Design template
14. Slide icon
15. Insertion point

a. A specific design, format, and color scheme that is applied to all the slides in a presentation
b. Indicates where your text will appear when you type in a text object
c. Determines how all of the elements on a slide are arranged
d. The slanted line border that appears around a text placeholder, indicating that it is ready to accept text
e. A box with a dashed border in which you can type text
f. In Outline view, the symbol that represents a slide

**Select the best answer from the list of choices.**

16. According to the unit, which of the following is *not* a guideline for planning a presentation?
    a. Determine the purpose of the presentation.
    b. Determine what you want to produce when the presentation is finished.
    c. Determine which type of output you need to best convey your message.
    d. Determine who else can give the final presentation.

17. Other than the Slide pane, where else can you enter slide text?
    a. Outline tab
    b. Print Preview
    c. Notes Page view
    d. Slides tab

18. Which of the following statements is *not* true?
    a. You can customize any PowerPoint template.
    b. The spellchecker identifies "there" as misspelled if the correct word for the context is "their".
    c. Speaker notes do not appear during the slide show.
    d. PowerPoint has many colorful templates from which to choose.

19. When you evaluate your presentation, you should make sure it follows which of the following criteria?
    a. The slides should include every piece of information to be presented so the audience can read it.
    b. The slides should use as many colors as possible to hold the audience's attention.
    c. Many different typefaces make the slides more interesting.
    d. The message should be clearly outlined without a lot of extra words.

20. What is the definition of a slide layout?
    a. A slide layout automatically applies all the objects you can use on a slide.
    b. A slide layout determines how all the elements on a slide are arranged.
    c. A slide layout applies a different template to the presentation.
    d. A slide layout puts all your slides in order.

21. When the spellchecker identifies a word as misspelled, which of the following is *not* a choice?
    a. To ignore this occurrence of the error
    b. To change the misspelled word to the correct spelling
    c. To have the spellchecker automatically correct all the errors it finds
    d. To ignore all occurrences of the error in the presentation

22. When you type text in a text placeholder, it becomes:
    a. A label.
    b. A title.
    c. A selection box.
    d. A text object.

# ▼ SKILLS REVIEW

1. **Enter slide text.**
   a. Start PowerPoint if necessary.
   b. In the Slide pane in Normal view, enter the text **Product Marketing** in the title placeholder.
   c. In the main text placeholder, enter **Rueben Agarpao**.
   d. On the next line of the placeholder, enter **Manager**.
   e. On the next line of the placeholder, enter **April 14, 2006**.
   f. Deselect the text object.
   g. Save the presentation as **RouterJet Tests** to the drive and folder where your Data Files are stored.

**2. Create new slides.**

  **a.** Create a new slide.

  **b.** Review the text in Table B-4, then select the appropriate slide layout.

  **c.** Enter the text from Table B-4 into the new slide.

  **d.** Create a new bulleted list slide using the Slide Layout task pane.

  **e.** Enter the text from Table B-5 into the new slide.

  **f.** Save your changes.

**3. Enter text in the Outline tab.**

  **a.** Open the Outline tab.

  **b.** Create a new bulleted list slide after the last one.

  **c.** Enter the text from Table B-6 into the new slide.

  **d.** Move the third bullet point in the second indent level to the second position.

  **e.** Switch back to the Slides tab.

  **f.** Save your changes.

**4. Add slide headers and footers.**

  **a.** Open the Header and Footer dialog box.

  **b.** Type today's date into the Fixed text box.

  **c.** Add the slide number to the footer.

  **d.** Type your name in the Footer text box.

  **e.** Apply the footer to all of the slides.

  **f.** Open the Header and Footer dialog box again, then click the Notes and Handouts tab.

  **g.** Enter today's date in the Fixed text box.

  **h.** Type the name of your class in the Header text box.

  **i.** Type your name in the Footer text box.

  **j.** Apply the header and footer information to all the notes and handouts.

  **k.** Save your changes.

**5. Choose a look for a presentation.**

  **a.** Open the Slide Design task pane.

  **b.** Locate the Profile template, then apply it to all the slides.

  **c.** Move to Slide 1.

  **d.** Locate the Pixel template, then apply it to Slide 1.

  **e.** Save your changes.

**6. Check spelling in a presentation.**

  **a.** Perform a spelling check on the document and change any misspelled words. Ignore any words that are correctly spelled but that the spellchecker doesn't recognize.

  **b.** Save your changes.

**7. Evaluate a presentation.**

  **a.** View Slide 1 in the Slide Show view, then move through the slide show.

  **b.** Evaluate the presentation using the points described in the lesson as criteria.

  **c.** Preview your presentation.

  **d.** Print the outline of the presentation.

  **e.** Print the slides of your presentation in grayscale with a frame around each slide.

  **f.** Save your changes, close the presentation, and exit PowerPoint.

**TABLE B-4**

| text object | text to insert |
| --- | --- |
| Slide title | RouterJet Project Tests - Rueben |
| First indent level | Focus: Component System |
| Second indent level | User access components |
| | Security components |
| | Network components |
| | System components |
| First indent level | Data Files and Report |
| Second indent level | Compile component data files |
| | Define component interface parameters |
| | Write function data report |

**TABLE B-5**

| text object | text to insert |
| --- | --- |
| Slide title | RouterJet Project Tests - Jeremy |
| First indent level | Focus: Network Integration |
| Second indent level | Server codes and routes |
| | File transfer |
| | Data conversion |
| | Platform functionality ratings |

**TABLE B-6**

| text object | text to insert |
| --- | --- |
| Slide title | RouterJet Project Tests - Nura |
| First indent level | Focus: Software QA |
| Second indent level | User access testing |
| | Software compatibility testing |
| | Platform testing |

# ▼ INDEPENDENT CHALLENGE 1

You have been asked to give a one-day course at a local adult education center. The course is called "Personal Computing for the Slightly Anxious Beginner" and is intended for adults who have never used a computer. One of your responsibilities is to create presentation slides that outline the course materials.

Plan and create presentation slides that outline the course material for the students. Create slides for the course introduction, course description, course text, grading policies, and a detailed syllabus. Create your own course material, but assume the following: the school has a computer lab with personal computers running Microsoft Windows software; each student has a computer; the prospective students are intimidated by computers but want to learn; and the course is on a Saturday from 9 a.m. to 5 p.m., with a one-hour lunch break.

   a. Write a short paragraph that explains the results you want to see, the information you need, and the type of message you want to communicate.
   b. Write an outline of your presentation. Indicate which content should go on each of the slides. Remember that your audience has never used computers before and needs computer terms defined.
   c. Start PowerPoint and create the presentation by entering the title slide text.
   d. Create the required slides as well as an ending slide that summarizes your presentation.

## Advanced Challenge Exercise

   ■ Open the Notes Page view.
   ■ To at least three slides, add notes that you want to remember when you give the class.
   ■ Print the Notes Page view for the presentation.

   e. Check the spelling in the presentation.
   f. Save the presentation as **Computer Class 101** to the drive and folder where your Data Files are stored.
   g. View the presentation in Slide Show view.
   h. Add your name as a footer on the notes and handouts, print handouts (six slides per page), and then print the presentation outline.
   i. Save your changes, close your presentation, then exit PowerPoint.

# ▼ INDEPENDENT CHALLENGE 2

You are the training director for Catch Up, Ltd., a German company in Berlin that coordinates special events, including corporate functions, weddings, and private parties. You regularly train groups of temporary employees that you can call on as coordinators, kitchen and wait staff, and coat checkers for specific events. The company trains 10 to 15 new workers each month for the peak season between May and September. One of your responsibilities is to orient new temporary employees at the next training session.

Plan and create presentation slides that outline your employee orientation. Create slides for the introduction, agenda, company history, dress requirements, principles for interacting successfully with guests, and safety requirements. Create your own presentation and company material, but assume the following: Catch Up, Ltd. is owned by Jan Negd-Sorenson; the new employee training class lasts four hours, and your orientation lasts 15 minutes; the training director's presentation lasts 15 minutes; and the dress code requires uniforms, supplied by Catch Up, Ltd. (white for daytime events, black and white for evening events).

   a. Think about the results you want to see, the information you need, and the message you want to communicate.
   b. Write a presentation outline. What content should go on the slides?
   c. Start PowerPoint and create the presentation by entering the slide text for all your slides.
   d. Create a slide that summarizes your presentation, then add an appropriate design template.
   e. Create an ending slide with the following information:
      **Catch Up, Ltd.**
      **Gubener Strasse 765, 10243 Berlin**
      **(Berlin-Friedrichshain)**
      **TEL.: 393795, FAX: 39375719**
   f. Check the spelling in the presentation.

# ▼ INDEPENDENT CHALLENGE 2 (CONTINUED)

**g.** Save the presentation as **Catch Up Training** to the drive and folder where your Data Files are stored.

**h.** View the slide show, then view the slides in Slide Sorter view. Evaluate your presentation; make any changes necessary so that the final version is focused, clear, concise, and readable.

**i.** Add your name as a footer on the notes and handouts, print the presentation as handouts (two slides per page), then print the presentation outline.

**j.** Save your changes, close your presentation, then exit PowerPoint.

# ▼ INDEPENDENT CHALLENGE 3

You are an independent distributor of natural foods in Albuquerque, New Mexico. Your business, All Natural Foods, has grown progressively since its inception eight years ago, but sales and profits have leveled off over the last nine months. In an effort to stimulate growth, you decide to acquire two major natural food dealers, which would allow All Natural Foods to expand its territory into surrounding states. Use PowerPoint to develop a presentation that you can use to gain a financial backer for the acquisition.

**a.** Start PowerPoint. Choose the Maple design template. Enter **Growth Plan** as the main title on the title slide, and **All Natural Foods** as the subtitle.

**b.** Save the presentation as **Growth Plan Proposal** to the drive and folder where your Data Files are stored.

**c.** Add five more slides with the following titles: Slide 2–Background; Slide 3–Current Situation; Slide 4–Acquisition Goals; Slide 5–Our Management Team; Slide 6–Funding Required.

**d.** Enter text into the text placeholders of the slides. Use both the Slide pane and the Outline tab to enter text.

**e.** Check the spelling in the presentation.

**f.** View the presentation as a slide show, then view the slides in Slide Sorter view.

**g.** Add your name as a footer on the notes and handouts, save your changes, then print handouts (six slides per page).

**h.** Close your presentation, then exit PowerPoint.

**Advanced Challenge Exercise**

- Create a new slide at the end of the presentation. Enter concluding text on the slide, summarizing the main points of the presentation.
- Apply at least one design template to the presentation.
- Evaluate your presentation using the points identified in the Evaluating a Presentation lesson. Use a word processor to write a short paragraph explaining how your presentation met the goals for proper presentation development.
- Make any changes you feel are necessary, then identify the changes and explain your reasoning in a word processing document.
- Save the presentation as **Growth Plan Proposal 2** to the drive and folder where your Data Files are stored.
- Print the presentation outline, close your presentation, then exit PowerPoint.

**FIGURE C-1:** New from Existing Presentation dialog box

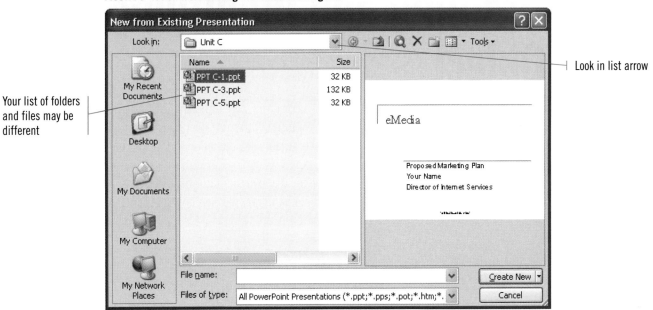

Your list of folders and files may be different

Look in list arrow

**FIGURE C-2:** First slide of the eMedia presentation

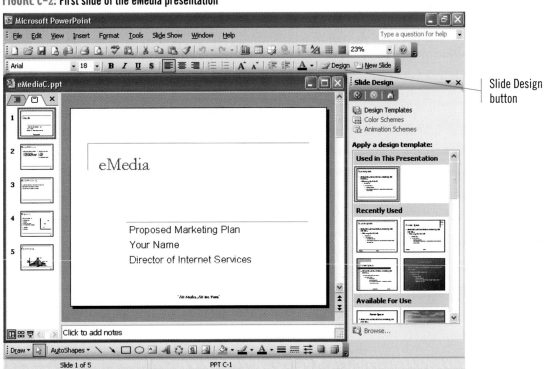

Slide Design button

## Clues to Use

### Setting permissions

In PowerPoint 2003, you can set specific access permissions for people who review or edit your work, so you have better control over your content. For example, you may want to give a user permission to edit or change your presentation but not allow them to print it. You can also restrict a user by permitting them to view the presentation, without the ability to edit or print the presentation, or you can give the user full access or control of the presentation. To set user access permissions, click the Permission button [icon] on the Standard toolbar. To use this feature, you have to first install the Windows Rights Management software.

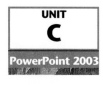

# Drawing and Modifying an Object

Using the drawing commands in PowerPoint, you can draw lines and shapes, and insert objects to enhance your presentation. The objects that you create or insert with the PowerPoint drawing tools can be modified to meet your design needs. The graphic attributes that you can change include fill color, line color, line style, shadow, and 3-D effects. To add drawn objects to your slides, use the buttons on the Drawing toolbar, which is typically docked at the bottom of the screen above the status bar. You decide to draw more objects on Slide 4 of your presentation to complete the graphic elements on the slide.

## STEPS

1. **In the Slides tab, click the Slide 4 thumbnail**
   Slide 4, titled "Competition", appears in the Slide pane.

2. **Press and hold [Shift], click the body text object, then release [Shift]**
   A dotted selection box with small circles called **sizing handles** appears around the text object. If you click a text object without pressing [Shift], a selection box composed of slanted lines appears, indicating that the object is active and ready to accept text, but it is not selected. When an object is selected, you can change its size, shape, or attributes by dragging one of the sizing handles.

   > **TROUBLE**
   > If you are not satisfied with the size of the text object, resize it again.

3. **Position the pointer over the right, middle sizing handle, the pointer changes to ↔, then drag the sizing handle to the left until the vertical line aligns with the top and bottom middle sizing handles**
   The text object is about half its original size, as shown in Figure C-3. When you position the pointer over a sizing handle, it changes to ↔. It points in different directions depending on which sizing handle it is positioned over. When you drag a sizing handle, the pointer changes to ┼, and a dotted outline appears, representing the size of the text object.

4. **Click the AutoShapes button [AutoShapes ▾] on the Drawing toolbar, point to Block Arrows, then click the Right Arrow button [⇨] (first row, first column)**
   After you select a shape from the AutoShapes menu and move the pointer over the slide, the pointer changes to ┼.

   > **TROUBLE**
   > If your arrow object is not approximately the same size as the one shown in Figure C-4, press [Shift] and drag one of the corner sizing handles to resize the object.

5. **Position ┼ in the blank area of the slide to the right of the text object and below the graph, press and hold [Shift], drag down and to the right to create an arrow object, as shown in Figure C-4, release [Shift], then release the mouse button**
   When you release the mouse button, an arrow object appears on the slide, filled with the default color and outlined with the default line style. Pressing [Shift] while you create the object maintains the object's proportions as you change its size.

6. **Click the Line Color list arrow [✎ ▾] on the Drawing toolbar, then point to the dark green color (fourth square from the left)**
   A ScreenTip appears identifying this color as the Follow Title Text Scheme Color.

7. **Click the dark green color**
   PowerPoint applies the green color to the selected arrow object's outline.

8. **Click the Fill Color list arrow [◇ ▾] on the Drawing toolbar, then click the white color (first square on the left, the Follow Background Scheme Color)**
   PowerPoint fills the selected arrow object with white.

9. **Click the Save button [💾] on the Standard toolbar to save your changes**

**FIGURE C-3:** Resizing a text object

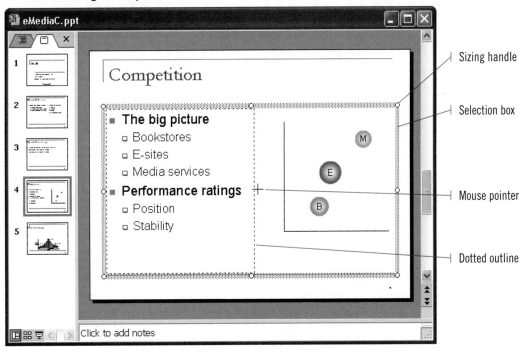

FIGURE C-3 labels: Sizing handle, Selection box, Mouse pointer, Dotted outline

**FIGURE C-4:** Arrow object on slide

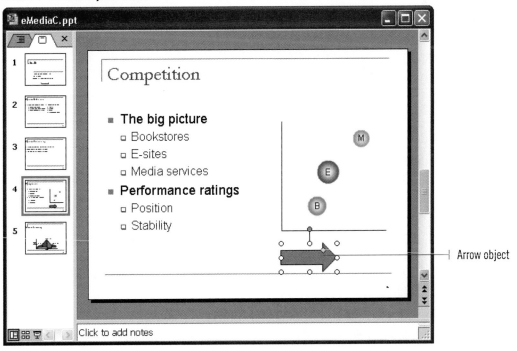

FIGURE C-4 label: Arrow object

## Clues to Use

### Understanding PowerPoint objects

In PowerPoint, you often work with multiple objects on the same slide. These may be text objects or graphic objects, such as drawn objects, clip art, or charts. To help you organize objects on a slide, you can align, group, and stack the objects using the Align or Distribute, Group, and Order commands on the Draw menu on the Drawing toolbar. When you align objects, you place their edges (or their centers) on the same plane. For example, you might want to align two squares vertically (one above the other) so that their left edges are in a straight vertical line. When you group objects, you combine two or more objects into one object. It's often helpful to group objects into one when you have finished positioning them on the slide. When you stack objects, you determine their order, that is, which ones are in front and which are in back. You can use the stacking order of objects to overlap them to create different effects.

# Editing Drawn Objects

In PowerPoint, you can easily change the size and shape of objects on a slide. You can alter the appearance of any object by dragging the sizing handles to adjust its dimensions. You can add text to most PowerPoint objects and you can move or copy objects. 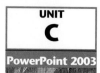 You want two arrows on Slide 4 that are the same shape and size. You first change the shape of the arrow object you've already drawn, and then you make a copy of it. Finally, you rotate one arrow to complete the graphic element.

## STEPS

1. **Click the arrow object to select it, if it is not already selected**

   In addition to sizing handles, two other handles appear on the selected object. You use the **adjustment handle**—a small yellow diamond—to change the appearance of an object. The adjustment handle appears next to the most prominent feature of the object, like the head of an arrow in this case. You use the **rotate handle**—a small green circle—to rotate the object.

   **TROUBLE**
   If you have trouble aligning the object in this step, press and hold [Alt] to turn off the snap to grid feature, then drag the object.

2. **Press and hold [Shift], drag the right, middle sizing handle on the arrow object to the right approximately ½", release [Shift], then release the mouse button**

3. **Position the pointer over the middle of the selected arrow object so that it changes to ↕, then drag the arrow object so that the arrow aligns with the horizontal axis of the chart as shown in Figure C-5**

   A dotted outline appears as you move the arrow object to help you position it. PowerPoint uses a hidden grid to align objects; it forces objects to "snap" to the grid lines. Make any adjustments to the arrow object position.

   **QUICK TIP**
   Rulers can help you align objects. To display the rulers, position the pointer in a blank area of the slide, right-click, then click Ruler on the shortcut menu.

4. **Position ↕ over the arrow object, then press and hold [Ctrl]**

   The pointer changes to ↖, indicating that PowerPoint makes a copy of the arrow object when you drag the mouse.

5. **Holding [Ctrl], drag the arrow object to the left until the dotted lines indicate that the arrow object copy is in a blank area of the slide, release [Ctrl], then release the mouse button**

   An identical copy of the arrow object appears on the slide.

6. **Type Price**

   The text appears in the center of the selected arrow object. The text is now part of the object, so if you move or rotate the object, the text moves with it.

   **QUICK TIP**
   You can also use the Rotate or Flip commands on the Draw button on the Drawing toolbar to rotate or flip objects 90 degrees.

7. **Position the pointer over the rotate handle of the selected arrow object so that it changes to ↻, then drag the rotate handle counterclockwise until the arrow head is pointing straight up**

   If you need to make any adjustments to the arrow object, drag the rotate handle again. Compare your screen with Figure C-6.

8. **Click the other arrow object, type Performance, then click in a blank area of the slide**

   Clicking a blank area of the slide deselects all objects that are selected.

9. **Click the Save button 🔲 on the Standard toolbar to save your changes**

**FIGURE C-5:** Slide showing resized arrow object

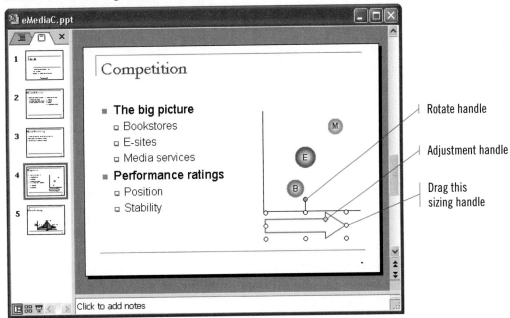

Rotate handle

Adjustment handle

Drag this sizing handle

**FIGURE C-6:** Slide showing duplicated arrow object

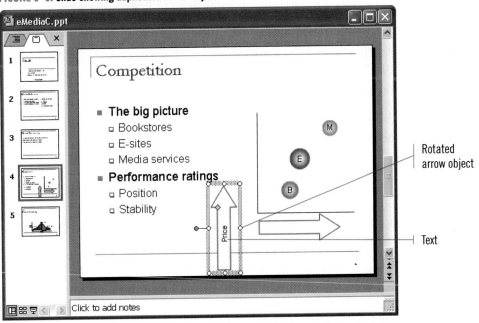

Rotated arrow object

Text

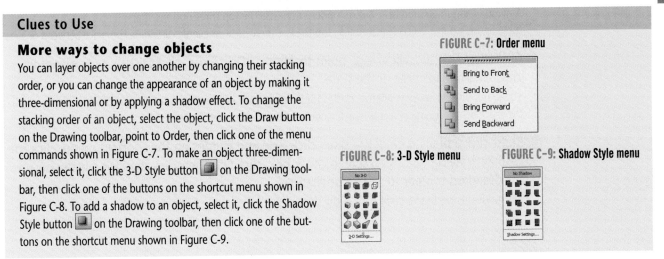

### Clues to Use

## More ways to change objects

You can layer objects over one another by changing their stacking order, or you can change the appearance of an object by making it three-dimensional or by applying a shadow effect. To change the stacking order of an object, select the object, click the Draw button on the Drawing toolbar, point to Order, then click one of the menu commands shown in Figure C-7. To make an object three-dimensional, select it, click the 3-D Style button 🔲 on the Drawing toolbar, then click one of the buttons on the shortcut menu shown in Figure C-8. To add a shadow to an object, select it, click the Shadow Style button 🔲 on the Drawing toolbar, then click one of the buttons on the shortcut menu shown in Figure C-9.

**FIGURE C-7:** Order menu

Bring to Front
Send to Back
Bring Forward
Send Backward

**FIGURE C-8:** 3-D Style menu

No 3-D

3-D Settings...

**FIGURE C-9:** Shadow Style menu

No Shadow

Shadow Settings...

PowerPoint 2003

# Aligning and Grouping Objects

After you create objects, modify their appearance, and edit their size and shape, you can position them on the slide, align them, distribute them, and then group them. The Align command arranges objects relative to each other by snapping the selected objects to a hidden grid of evenly spaced vertical and horizontal lines. The Distribute command evenly distributes the space horizontally or vertically between selected objects. The Group command groups objects into one object, which makes retaining their relative position easy while editing and moving them.  You are ready to position and group the arrow objects on Slide 4 and then align and distribute some other objects with which you have been working.

## STEPS

1. **Right-click a blank area of the slide, then click Grid and Guides on the shortcut menu**

   The Grid and Guides dialog box opens.

2. **Click the Display drawing guides on screen check box, then click OK**

   The PowerPoint guides appear as dotted lines on the slide. (The dotted lines may be very faint on your screen.) The guides intersect at the center of the slide. They help you position the arrow object.

3. **Position ↖ over the vertical guide in a blank area of the slide, press and hold the mouse button until the pointer changes to a guide measurement, then drag the guide to the right until the guide measurement box reads approximately 1.00**

4. **Position ⟨ over the Price arrow object, then drag it so that the right edge of the selection box touches the vertical guide as shown in Figure C-10**

   The arrow object attaches or "snaps" to the vertical guide.

5. **With the Price arrow object selected, press and hold [Shift], click the Performance arrow object, then release [Shift]**

   The two objects are now selected.

6. **Click the Draw button Draw ▾ on the Drawing toolbar, then click Group**

   The arrow objects group to form one object without losing their individual attributes. Notice the sizing handles and rotate handle now appear on the outer edge of the grouped object, not around each individual object.

7. **In the Slides tab, click the Slide 5 thumbnail, press and hold [Shift], click each of the five graph object shapes, then release [Shift]**

   The five graph object shapes are selected.

8. **Click Draw ▾, then point to Align or Distribute**

   A menu of alignment and distribution options appears. The top three options align objects vertically; the next three options align objects horizontally; and the last three options evenly distribute the space between objects.

9. **Click Align Bottom, click Draw ▾, point to Align or Distribute, click Distribute Horizontally, then click a blank area of the slide**

   The graph objects are now aligned horizontally along their bottom edges and are distributed evenly so that the space between each object is equal. Compare your screen with Figure C-11.

10. **Right-click a blank area of the slide, click Grid and Guides on the shortcut menu, click the Display drawing guides on screen check box, click OK, then click the Save button 🖫 on the Standard toolbar to save your changes**

    The guides are no longer displayed on the slide.

**FIGURE C-10:** Repositioned arrow object

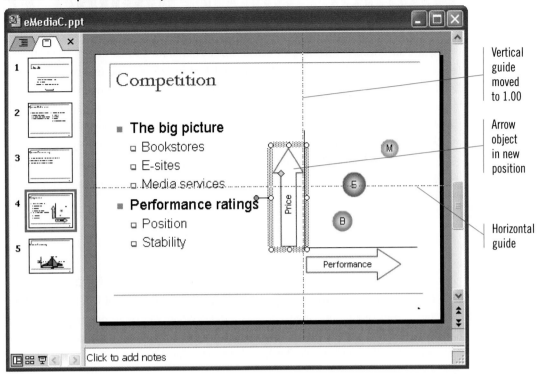

Vertical guide moved to 1.00

Arrow object in new position

Horizontal guide

**FIGURE C-11:** Aligned and distributed graph objects

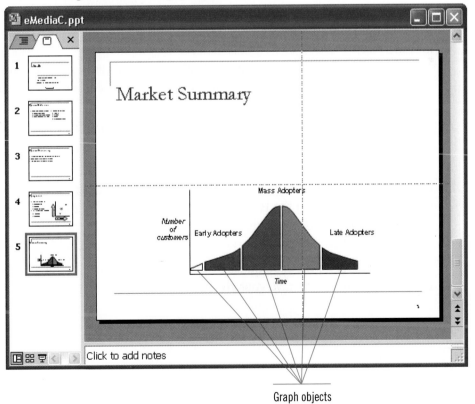

Graph objects

# Adding and Arranging Text

Using the advanced text-editing capabilities of PowerPoint, you can easily type, insert, or rearrange text. The PowerPoint slide layouts allow you to enter text in prearranged text placeholders. If these text place-holders don't provide the flexibility you need, you can use the Text Box button on the Drawing toolbar to create your own text objects. With the Text Box button, you can create two types of text objects: a text label, used for a small phrase where text doesn't automatically wrap to the next line inside the box; and a word processing box, used for a sentence or paragraph where the text wraps inside the boundaries of the box.  You decide that Slide 5 needs a little more information to make it complete. Use the Text Box button to create a word processing box to enter information about the graph chart that is on the slide.

## STEPS

1. **Click the Text Box button 🔳 on the Drawing toolbar**
   The pointer changes to ↓.

2. **Position ↓ near the left side of the slide, above the top of the chart, then drag down and toward the right side of the slide about an inch and a half to create a word processing box**
   Your screen should look similar to Figure C-12. When you begin dragging, an outline of the text object appears, indicating how large a text object you are drawing. After you release the mouse button, an insertion point appears inside the text object, ready to accept text.

3. **Type Changes in market, costs, share, pricing, and competition**
   Notice that the text object increases in size as your text wraps inside the text object. There is a mistake in the text. It should read "market share".

4. **Double-click the word share to select it**

5. **Position the pointer on top of the selected word and press and hold the mouse button**
   The pointer changes to ▨.

6. **Drag the word share to the right of the word market in the text object, then release the mouse button**
   A dotted insertion line appears as you drag, indicating where PowerPoint places the word when you release the mouse button. The word "share" moves next to the word "market". Moving the word "share" leaves an extra comma, which you need to delete.

7. **Position I to the right of one of the commas after the word "costs", then press [Backspace]**
   One of the commas is deleted.

8. **Drag the right-middle sizing handle of the text object to the right until the word "costs" moves to the top line of the text object, position ▨ over the text object border, then drag it to the center of the slide**
   Your screen should look similar to Figure C-13.

9. **Click a blank area of the slide outside the text object, then click the Save button 🔳 on the Standard toolbar to save your changes**

**FIGURE C-12:** Word processing box ready to accept text

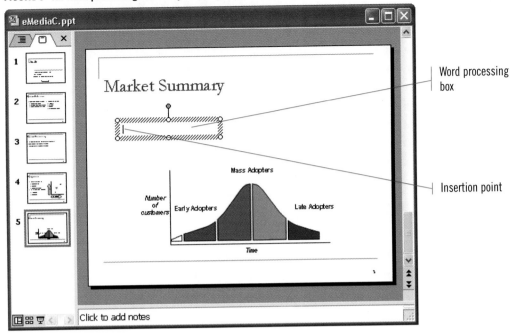

Word processing box

Insertion point

**FIGURE C-13:** Text added to the word processing box

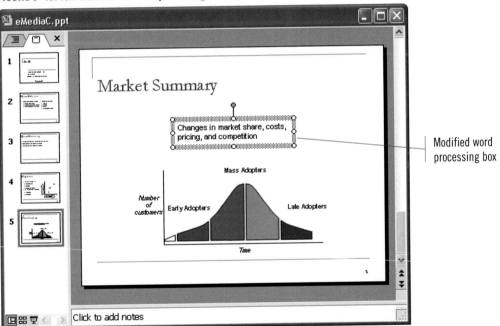

Modified word processing box

## Clues to Use

### Review a presentation

You can send a copy of a presentation over the Internet to others for them to review, edit, and add comments. To send your presentation out for review, you can use Microsoft Outlook, which automatically tracks changes made by reviewers, or you can use any other compatible e-mail program. To send a presentation to reviewers using Outlook, click File on the menu bar, point to Send To, then click Mail Recipient (for Review). Outlook opens and automatically creates a "Review Request" e-mail with the PowerPoint presentation attached to it for you to send to reviewers. Reviewers can use any version of PowerPoint to review, edit, and comment on their copy of your presentation. Once a reviewer is finished with the presentation and sends it back to you, you can combine their changes and comments with your original presentation using the PowerPoint Compare and Merge Presentations feature. When you do this, the Revisions task pane opens with commands that allow you to accept or reject reviewers' changes.

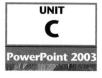

# Formatting Text

Once you have entered and arranged the text in your presentation, you can modify the way the text looks to emphasize your message. Important text needs to be highlighted in some way to distinguish it from other text or objects on the slide. Less important information does not need to be emphasized. For example, if you have two text objects on the same slide, you could draw attention to one text object by changing its color or size. To change the way text looks, you need to select it, then choose a Formatting command. In this lesson, you use some of the commands on the Formatting and Drawing toolbars to change the way the new text object looks on Slide 5.

## STEPS

**1. On Slide 5, press [Shift], then click the new text object**

The entire text object is selected. Any changes you make affect all the text in the selected text object. Changing the text's size and appearance helps emphasize it. When a text object is already selected because you have been entering text in it, you can select the entire text object by clicking on its border with ⬚.

**2. Click the Increase Font Size button Å on the Formatting toolbar twice**

The text increases in size to 24 points. The size of the font is listed in the Font Size text box on the Formatting toolbar.

**3. Click the Italic button I on the Formatting toolbar**

The text changes from normal to italic text. The Italic and Bold buttons are toggle buttons, which you click to turn the attribute on or off.

**4. Click the Font Color list arrow A ▾ on the Formatting toolbar**

The Font Color menu appears, showing the eight colors used in the current presentation and the More Colors command, which lets you choose additional colors.

**5. Click More Colors to open the Colors dialog box, then click the teal cell in the upper-left corner of the color hexagon, second from the left, as shown in Figure C-14**

The Current color and the New color appear in the box in the lower-right corner of the dialog box.

**6. Click OK**

The text in the text object changes to teal, and the teal color is added as the ninth color in the set of colors used in the presentation.

**7. Click the Font list arrow on the Formatting toolbar**

A list of available fonts opens with Arial, the font used in the text object, selected in the list.

**8. Click the down scroll arrow, then click Times New Roman**

The Times New Roman font replaces the original font in the text object.

**9. Click the Center button ≡ on the Formatting toolbar, then resize the text object so that the word "costs" is on the top line in the text object**

The text is aligned in the center of the text object and is contained on two lines.

**10. Drag the text object so it is centered over the chart, click a blank area of the slide outside the text object to deselect it, then click the Save button 🖫 on the Standard toolbar**

Compare your screen to Figure C-15.

FIGURE C-14: Colors dialog box

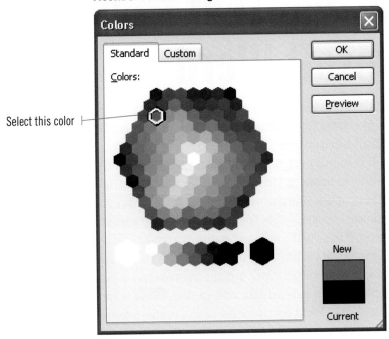

Select this color

FIGURE C-15: Slide showing formatted text object

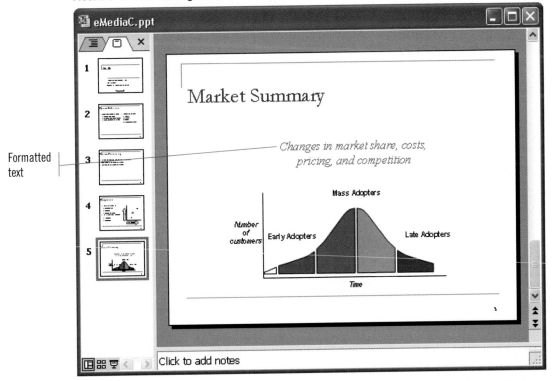

Formatted text

## Clues to Use

### Replacing text and attributes

As you review your presentation, you may decide to replace certain words throughout the entire presentation. You can automatically modify words, sentences, text case, and periods. To replace specific words or sentences, click Edit on the menu bar, then click Replace. To automatically add or remove periods from title or body text and to automatically change the case of title or body text, click Tools on the menu bar, click Options, click the Spelling and Style tab, then click Style Options to open the Style Options dialog box. Specify the options you want on the Case and End Punctuation tab. The options on the Visual Clarity tab in the Style Options dialog box control the legibility of bulleted text items on the slides.

PowerPoint 2003

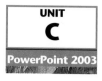
# Importing Text from Microsoft Word

PowerPoint makes it easy to insert information from other sources, such as Microsoft Word, into a presentation. If you have an existing Word document or outline, you can import it into PowerPoint to create a new presentation or insert additional slides in an existing presentation. Documents saved in Microsoft Word format (.doc), Rich Text Format (.rtf), plain text format (.txt), and HTML format (.htm) can be inserted into a presentation. When you import a Microsoft Word or a Rich Text Format document into a presentation, PowerPoint creates an outline structure based on the styles in the document. For example, a Heading 1 style in the Word document becomes a slide title in PowerPoint and a Heading 2 style becomes the first level of text in a bulleted list. If you insert a plain text format document into a presentation, PowerPoint creates an outline based on the tabs at the beginning of the document's paragraphs. Paragraphs without tabs become slide titles; paragraphs with one tab indent become first-level text in bulleted lists; paragraphs with two tabs become second-level text in bulleted lists; and so on. One of your colleagues from the Sales Department has sent you a Word document containing further information that you need for your presentation. You insert this document into your presentation.

## STEPS

1. **Click the Outline tab, then click the up scroll arrow in the Outline tab until the Slide 4 slide title appears**

2. **Click the Slide 4 icon**
   Slide 4 appears in the Slide pane. Each time you click a slide icon in the Outline tab, the slide title and text are highlighted indicating the slide is selected. Before you insert information into a presentation, you must first designate where you want the information to be placed. In this case, the Word document is inserted after Slide 4, the selected slide.

3. **Click Insert on the menu bar, then click Slides from Outline**
   The Insert Outline dialog box opens.

4. **Locate the Word document PPT C-2.doc in the drive and folder where your Data Files are stored, then click Insert**
   Three new slides (5, 6, and 7) are added to the presentation. See Figure C-16. Slide 5 is selected showing you where the information from the Word document begins.

5. **Read the text for the new Slide 5 in the Slide pane, click the down scroll arrow in the Outline tab until the Slide 8 icon is displayed, click the Slide 6 icon in the Outline tab, then review the text on that slide**
   Slide 6 is selected; you can see the text for Slide 7 in the Outline tab.

6. **Click the Slides tab, then click the Slide 7 thumbnail**
   After reviewing the text on this slide, you realize that someone else is covering this information in another presentation.

7. **Right-click the Slide 7 thumbnail, then click Delete Slide on the shortcut menu**
   Slide 7 is deleted from the presentation. The last slide in the presentation, Market Summary, now appears in the Slide pane. Compare your screen to Figure C-17.

8. **Click the Save button on the Standard toolbar to save your changes**

FIGURE C-16: Outline tab showing imported text

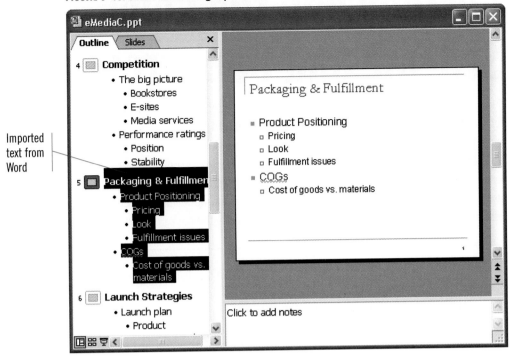

Imported text from Word

FIGURE C-17: Presentation after deleting slide

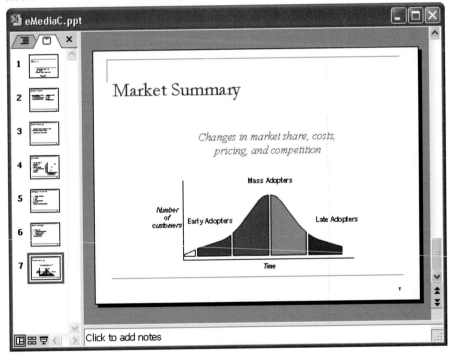

## Clues to Use

### Inserting slides from other presentations

To insert slides into the current presentation, click Insert on the menu bar, then click Slides from Files. Click Browse in the Slide Finder dialog box, then locate the presentation from which you want to copy slides. In the Select slides section, select the slide(s) you want to insert, click Insert, then click Close. The new slides automatically take on the design of the current presentation. If both presentations are open, you can copy the slides from one presentation to another. Change the view of each presentation to Slide Sorter view, select the desired slides, then copy and paste them (or use drag and drop) into the desired presentation. You can then rearrange the slides in Slide Sorter view if necessary.

# Customizing the Color Scheme and Background

Every PowerPoint presentation has a **color scheme**, a set of eight coordinated colors that determine the colors for the slide elements in your presentation: slide background, text and lines, shadows, title text, fills, accents, and hyperlinks. The design template that is applied to a presentation determines its color scheme. See Table C-1 for a description of the slide color scheme elements. The **background** is the area behind the text and graphics. Every design template in PowerPoint—even the blank presentation template—has a color scheme that you can use or modify. You can change the background color and appearance independently of changing the color scheme. You change the color scheme and modify the background of the presentation.

## STEPS

**QUICK TIP**

To apply a new color scheme to only selected slides, select the slides on the Slides tab or in Slide Sorter view, point to the color scheme in the Slide Design task pane, click the list arrow that appears, then click Apply to Selected Slides.

1. **Click the Color Schemes hyperlink in the Slide Design task pane**
   The current, or default, color scheme is selected with a blue border as shown in Figure C-18. Additional color schemes designed specifically for the applied design template (in this case, the Edge template) are also shown.

2. **Click the color scheme icon in the fourth row, second column in the Slide Design task pane**
   The new color scheme is applied to all the slides in the presentation. In this case, the new color scheme changes the color of the slide graphics and title text, but the bulleted text and background remain the same.

3. **Click Format on the menu bar, then click Background**
   The Background dialog box opens.

4. **In the Background fill section, click the list arrow below the preview of the slide, click Fill Effects, then click the Gradient tab, if it is not already selected**

**QUICK TIP**

If you click the Preset option button, you can choose from a variety of predesigned backgrounds. You can also add other backgrounds by clicking one of the other tabs in the Fill Effects dialog box.

5. **Click the One color option button in the Colors section, click the Color 1 list arrow, then click the olive green color (the Follow Accent Scheme Color)**
   The green color fills the Color 1 list arrow and the four variant colors preview in the Variants section, showing that the background is shaded with green.

6. **Drag the Brightness scroll box all the way to the right (toward Light) in the Colors section, click the Diagonal down option button in the Shading Styles section, then click the lower-left variant**
   The four variant previews change shading. Compare your screen to Figure C-19.

**QUICK TIP**

You can also apply a shaded background to an AutoShape by right-clicking the object, then clicking Format Autoshape in the shortcut menu.

7. **Click OK, then click Apply to All**
   The slide background is now shaded from green to white and then green again.

8. **Click the Slide Sorter View button ⊞, click the Zoom list arrow on the Standard toolbar, then click 50%**
   The final presentation appears in Slide Sorter view. Compare your screen to Figure C-20.

9. **Add your name as a footer on the notes and handouts, print the slides as handouts (4 slides per page), click the Save button 🖫, close the presentation, then exit PowerPoint**

**FIGURE C-18: Slide Design task pane**

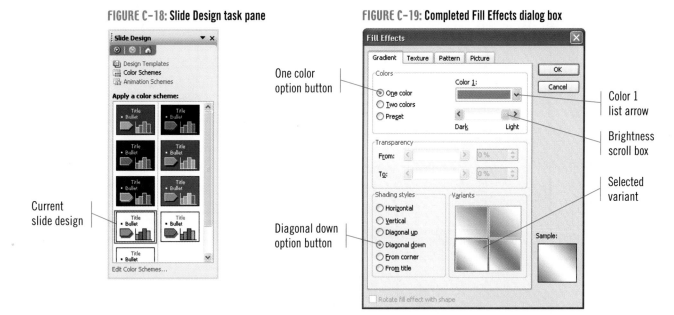

Current slide design

**FIGURE C-19: Completed Fill Effects dialog box**

One color option button

Color 1 list arrow

Brightness scroll box

Selected variant

Diagonal down option button

**FIGURE C-20: Final presentation in Slide Sorter view**

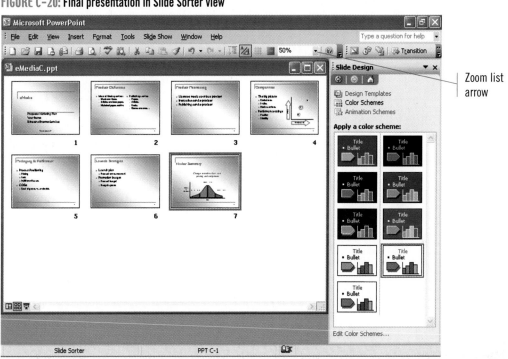

Zoom list arrow

**TABLE C-1: Color scheme elements**

| scheme element | description |
| --- | --- |
| Background color | Color of the slide's canvas or background |
| Text and lines color | Used for text and drawn lines; contrasts with the background color |
| Shadows color | Color of the shadow of the text or other object; generally a darker shade of the background color |
| Title text color | Used for slide title; like the text and line colors, contrasts with the background color |
| Fills color | Contrasts with both the background and the text and line colors |
| Accent colors | Colors used for other objects on slides, such as bullets |
| Accent and hyperlink colors | Colors used for accent objects and for hyperlinks you insert |
| Accent and followed hyperlink color | Color used for accent objects and for hyperlinks after they have been clicked |

# Practice

## ▼ CONCEPTS REVIEW

**Label each element of the PowerPoint window shown in Figure C-21.**

FIGURE C-21

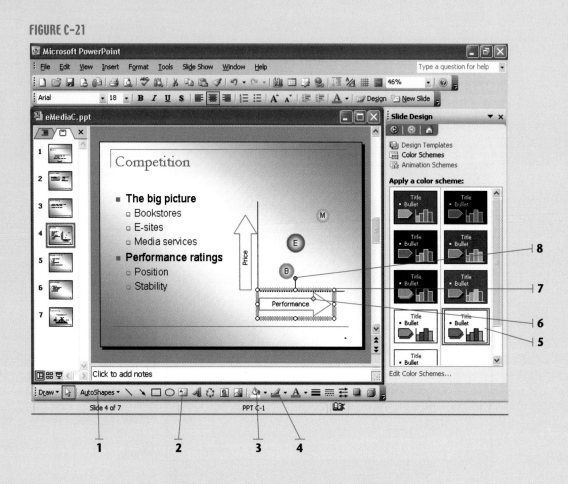

**Match each term or button with the statement that best describes it.**

9. **Sizing handle**          a. A text object for a word or small phrase

10. **Guide**                     b. A dotted line that helps you position objects

11. **Text label**              c. The area behind the text and graphics of a slide

12. **Color scheme**        d. Used to change the size and shape of an object

13. **Background**            e. A set of eight coordinated colors

## Select the best answer from the list of choices.

**14. What is the easiest way to line objects along their tops on a slide?**

   **a.** Group the objects together

   **b.** Use PowerPoint anchor lines

   **c.** Place the objects on the edge of the slide

   **d.** Use the Align Top command

**15. What does *not* happen when you group objects?**

   **a.** Sizing handles appear around the grouped object.

   **b.** Objects are grouped together as a single object.

   **c.** Objects lose their individual characteristics.

   **d.** The grouped objects have a rotate handle.

**16. What is *not* true about guides?**

   **a.** You can drag a guide off the slide to delete it.

   **b.** A PowerPoint guide is a dotted line.

   **c.** Slides can have only one vertical and one horizontal guide.

   **d.** You can press [Ctrl] and drag a guide to create a new one.

**17. What is *not* true about a presentation color scheme?**

   **a.** Every presentation has a color scheme.

   **b.** There are eight colors to every color scheme.

   **c.** You can't change the background color without changing the color scheme.

   **d.** The color scheme determines the colors of a slide.

**18. How do you change the size of a PowerPoint object?**

   **a.** Click the Resize button.

   **b.** Drag a sizing handle.

   **c.** Drag the rotate handle.

   **d.** You can't change the size of a PowerPoint object.

**19. What would you use to position objects at a specific place on a slide?**

   **a.** PowerPoint lines

   **b.** PowerPoint anchor lines

   **c.** PowerPoint placeholders

   **d.** PowerPoint guides and rulers

**20. PowerPoint objects can be:**

   **a.** Grouped and aligned.

   **b.** Converted to pictures.

   **c.** Distributed evenly.

   **d.** Both A and C.

**21. What is a slide background?**

   **a.** The slide grid

   **b.** The area behind text and graphics

   **c.** A picture

   **d.** The pasteboard off the slide

**22. What does the adjustment handle do?**

   **a.** Changes the angle adjustment of an object

   **b.** Changes the appearance of an object

   **c.** Adjusts the position of an object

   **d.** Adjusts the size of an object

# ▼ SKILLS REVIEW

## 1. Open an existing presentation.

**a.** Start PowerPoint.

**b.** Open the file **PPT C-3.ppt** from the drive and folder where your Data Files are stored.

**c.** Save it as **Product Report.ppt** to the drive and folder where your Data Files are stored.

## 2. Draw and modify an object.

**a.** Click Slide 4 in the Slides tab, insert the Left-Right-Up Arrow AutoShape from the Block Arrows category on the AutoShapes menu to the blank area on the slide.

**b.** Open the Line Color menu, click More Line Colors, then click the black color cell in the Colors dialog box to make the line color black.

**c.** Change the fill color to light green (the Follow Accent Scheme Color).

**d.** Rotate the arrow object so that the middle arrow-head points to the right. (*Hint*: 90° to the right.)

**e.** Use the arrows' sizing handles to adjust the size of the object until it matches Figure C-22.

**f.** Move the arrow object on the slide so that it is in the center of the blank space on the slide.

**g.** Deselect the arrow object, then save your changes.

FIGURE C-22

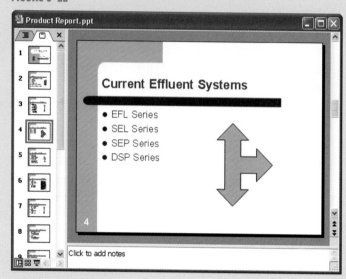

## 3. Edit drawn objects.

**a.** Select Slide 9, resize the arrow object so it is about ½" shorter. (*Hint*: You might want to resize the bulleted list text object so it does not interfere with your work.)

**b.** Drag the arrow object next to the left side of the box.

**c.** Use the adjustment handle to lengthen the arrow object's head about ¼", then insert the text **Satisfaction**. Enlarge the arrow object so that all the text fits inside it, if necessary.

**d.** Make two copies of the arrow object and arrange them to the left of the first one so that they are pointing in succession toward the box.

**e.** Drag to select the word **Satisfaction** on the middle arrow object, then type the word **Growth**.

**f.** Replace the word **Satisfaction** on the left arrow object with the word **Products**.

**g.** Insert the word **Success** in the cube object.

**h.** Change the text font for each of the objects to Arial italic. Enlarge the cube as necessary so the word **Success** fits in it.

**i.** Save your changes.

## 4. Align and group objects.

**a.** Align the middles of the four objects, then horizontally distribute the objects.

**b.** Group the arrow objects and the cube together.

**c.** Display the guides, then move the vertical guide left so the box displays 4.17; move the horizontal guide down to display 3.08.

**d.** Align the grouped object so its lower-left sizing handle snaps to where the guides intersect. (*Hint*: If your object does not snap to the guides, open the Grid and Guides dialog box, and make sure the Snap objects to grid check box is checked.)

**e.** Hide the guides, then save your changes. Compare your screen with Figure C-23.

FIGURE C-23

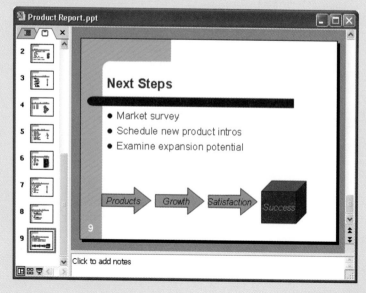

**5. Add and arrange text.**

 **a.** Add the text **Next steps** as a fourth item to the body text box on Slide 2.

 **b.** Near the bottom of the slide, below the graphic, create a word processing box about 3" wide, and in it enter the text: **The Future of Water Systems and Pumps**.

 **c.** Drag the word **Pumps** to the right of the word **Water**.

 **d.** Delete the word **and** and then the letter **s** on the word Pumps. The text object should now read, The Future of Water Pump Systems.

 **e.** Adjust the size of the text object to fit the text, then move the text object so that it is directly under the graphic.

 **f.** Save your changes.

**6. Format text.**

 **a.** Select the text object so that formatting commands apply to all the text in the object.

 **b.** Change the font color to the dark green color (the Follow Title Text Scheme Color), increase the font size to 24 points, then, if necessary, resize the word processing box so the text fits on one line.

 **c.** Change the text style to Italic, then align the words to the center of the text object.

 **d.** Click Slide 9 in the Slides tab, select the text in the cube, then change the font color to a light fluorescent green. (*Hint*: Use the Colors dialog box.)

 **e.** Click Slide 1 in the Slides tab, select the top title text font (Hildebrand Water Systems), then change the font size to 44.

 **f.** Deselect the text object, then save your changes.

**7. Import text from Microsoft Word.**

 **a.** Click Slide 9 in the Slides tab.

 **b.** Import the Word file PPT C-4.doc. Check the formatting of each of the three new slides—slides 10, 11, and 12.

 **c.** In the Slides tab, drag Slide 8 below Slide 11.

 **d.** In the Slides tab, delete Slide 9, Market Surveys.

 **e.** Save your changes.

**8. Customize the color scheme and background.**

 **a.** Open the Slide Design task pane and click the Color Schemes hyperlink.

 **b.** Apply the top right color scheme in the list to all the slides.

 **c.** Open the Background dialog box, then open the Fill Effects dialog box.

 **d.** On the Gradient tab, select the One color option, click the Color 1 list arrow, then click the yellow color.

 **e.** Drag the Brightness scroll box almost all the way to the right, select the From corner shading style and the lower-right variant.

 **f.** Apply this background to all slides.

 **g.** Add your name as a footer to the notes and handouts.

 **h.** Save your changes, then print the slides as handouts (4 slides per page).

 **i.** Close the file and exit PowerPoint.

# ▼ INDEPENDENT CHALLENGE 1

In this unit, you learned that when you work with multiple objects on a PowerPoint slide, there are ways to arrange them so your information appears neat and well organized. Using a word processing program, write a summary explaining how to perform each of these tasks in PowerPoint. Make sure you explain what happens to the objects when you perform these tasks. Also explain *why* you would perform these tasks.

   **a.** Start your word processor, open a new document, then save the file as **Arranging Objects** to the drive and folder where your Data Files are stored.

   **b.** Explain the six different ways to align objects.

   **c.** Explain what the Distribute command does.

   **d.** Explain the concept of grouping objects.

   **e.** Add your name as the first line in the document, save your changes, print the document, close the document, then exit the word processor.

# ▼ INDEPENDENT CHALLENGE 2

You work for Language Systems, a major producer of language-teaching CD-ROMs with accompanying instructional books. Twice a year the company holds title meetings to determine the new title list for the following production term and to decide which current CD titles need to be revised. As the director of acquisitions, you chair the September Title Meeting and present the basic material for discussion.

   **a.** Start PowerPoint, open the file PPT C-5.ppt from the drive and folder where your Data Files are stored, and save it as **2006 Title Meeting**.

   **b.** Add an appropriate design template to the presentation.

   **c.** After Slide 6, Insert the Word outline PPT C-6.doc that contains different product titles.

   **d.** Examine all of the slides in the presentation and apply italic formatting to all product and book titles.

   **e.** Format the text so that the most important information is the most prominent.

   **f.** Add appropriate shapes that emphasize the most important parts of the slide content. Format the objects using color and shading. Use the Align or Distribute and Group commands to organize your shapes.

**Advanced Challenge Exercise**

   ■ Using the AutoShapes menu, draw a shape from the Block Arrows menu, then apply 3-D Style 12 to the object using the 3-D Styles button.

   ■ Format at least one object with Shadow Style 2 using the Shadow Styles button on the Drawing toolbar.

   **g.** Spell check, view the final slide show, and evaluate your presentation. Make any necessary changes.

   **h.** Add your name as footer text on the notes and handouts, save the presentation, print the slides as handouts, close the file, and exit PowerPoint.

# ▼ INDEPENDENT CHALLENGE 3

The Learning Company is dedicated to the design and development of instructional software that helps college students learn software applications. You need to design four new logos for the company that incorporate the new company slogan: Software is a snap! The marketing group will decide which of the four designs looks best. Create your own presentation slides, but assume that the company colors are blue and green.

    **a.** Sketch your logos and slogan designs on a piece of paper. What text and graphics do you need for the slides?

    **b.** Start PowerPoint, create a new blank presentation, and save it as **Software Learning** to the drive and folder where your Data Files are stored.

    **c.** Create four different company logos, each one on a separate slide. Use the shapes on the AutoShapes menu, and enter the company slogan using the Text tool. (*Hint*: Use the Title only layout.) The logo and the marketing slogan should match each other in tone, size, and color; and the logo objects should be grouped together to make it easier for other employees to copy and paste.

    **d.** Format the fill color, line color, and fonts appropriately using the commands on the Formatting and Drawing toolbars.

### Advanced Challenge Exercise

    ■ Create at least one arrow object using the Arrow button and one line object using the Line button on the Drawing toolbar.

    ■ Use the Line Style button and Dash Style button on the Drawing toolbar to format objects.

    ■ Format an arrow object with the Arrow Style button on the Drawing toolbar.

    **e.** Spell check, view the final slide show, and evaluate your presentation.

    **f.** Add your name as footer text, save the presentation, print the slides and notes pages (if any), close the file, and exit PowerPoint.

# ▼ INDEPENDENT CHALLENGE 4

Your company is planning to offer 401(k) retirement plans to all its employees. The Human Resources Department has asked you to construct and deliver a brief presentation about 401(k) plans to employees. To find the necessary information for the presentation, you decide to use the Web. The information you find on the Web should answer the following questions:

    • What is a 401(k) plan?

    • How does a 401(k) plan work?

    • How much can I contribute to my 401(k) plan at work?

    • When do I have to start taking money from my 401(k) account?

    • Is there a penalty for early withdrawal?

    **a.** Connect to the Internet, then use a search engine to locate Web sites that have information on 401(k) plans.

    **b.** Review at least two Web sites that contain information about 401(k) plans. Print the Home pages of the Web sites you use to gather data for your presentation.

    **c.** Start PowerPoint. On the title slide, title the presentation **401(k) Plans: What Employees Need to Know**. The presentation should contain at least five slides, including the title slide. Refer to the bulleted list above as you create your content.

    **d.** Save the presentation as **401k Plans** to the drive and folder where your Data Files are stored.

    **e.** Apply a design template to the presentation, then customize the slide background.

    **f.** Use text formatting as necessary to make text visible and help emphasize important points.

    **g.** At least one slide should contain an object from the AutoShapes menu. Customize the object's size and color.

    **h.** Add your name as a footer to the slides, spell check the presentation, and view the final presentation.

    **i.** Save the final version of the presentation, print the slides, then close the file, and exit PowerPoint.

# ▼ VISUAL WORKSHOP

Create a one-slide presentation for SASLtd, a London-based company, that looks like the one shown in Figure C-24. Use a text box for each group heading. Group the objects in the lower-right logo. (*Hint*: The top-left rectangle object uses an option from the 3-D menu.) If you don't have the exact fonts, use something similar. Add your name as footer on the slide, save the presentation as **SASLtd** to the drive and folder where your Data Files are stored, then print the slide.

FIGURE C-24

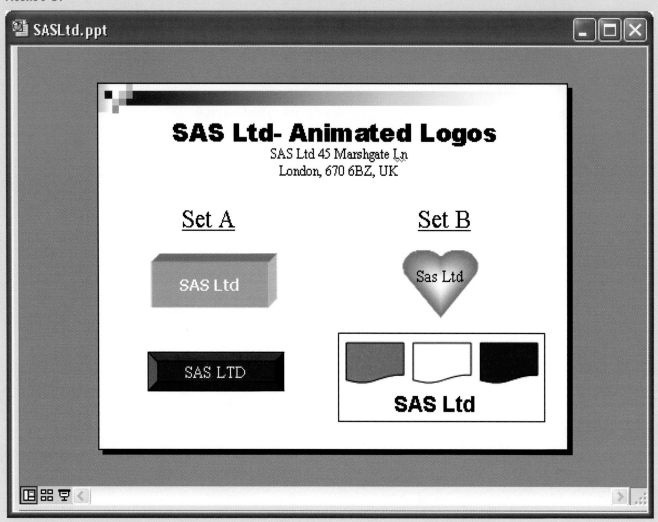

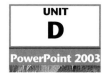

# Enhancing a Presentation

## OBJECTIVES

| |
|---|
| Insert clip art |
| Insert, crop, and scale a picture |
| Embed a chart |
| Enter and edit data in the datasheet |
| Format a chart |
| Create tables in PowerPoint |
| Use slide show commands |
| Set slide show timings and transitions |
| Set slide animation effects |

If you have a SAM user profile, you may have access to hands-on instruction, practice, and assessment of the skills covered in this unit. Log in to your SAM account and go to your assignments page to see what your instructor has assigned.

After completing the content of your presentation, you can supplement your slide text with clip art, photographs, charts, and other visual elements that help communicate your message and keep your presentation visually interesting. In this unit, you learn how to insert three of the most common visual elements: a clip art image, a picture, and a chart. These objects are created in other programs. After you add the objects, you rehearse the slide show and add special effects. ▀▀▀▀ You made changes to the eMedia presentation based on feedback from colleagues. Now you want to revise the presentation to make it easier to understand and more interesting to watch.

# Inserting Clip Art

PowerPoint has ready access to many professionally designed images, called **clip art**, that you can place in your presentation. Using clip art is the easiest and fastest way to enhance a presentation. In Microsoft Office, clip art and other media files, including photographs, movies, and sounds, are stored in a file index system called the Microsoft Clip Organizer. The Clip Organizer sorts the clip art into groups, including My Collections, Office Collections, and Web Collections. The Office Collections group holds all the media files that come with Microsoft Office. You can customize the Clip Organizer by adding clips to a collection, moving clips from one collection to another, or creating a new collection. As with drawing objects, you can modify clip art images by changing their shape, size, fill, or shading. Clip art is available from many sources outside the Clip Organizer, including the Microsoft Office Online Web site and collections on CD-ROMs. 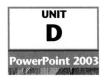 Add a picture from the Clip Organizer to one of the slides and then adjust its size and placement.

## STEPS

1.  **Start PowerPoint, open the presentation PPT D-1.ppt from the drive and folder where your Data Files are stored, save it as eMediaD, click View on the menu bar, click Task Pane, click Window on the menu bar, then click Arrange All**

2.  **Click Slide 8 in the Slides tab, then click the Insert Clip Art button 🖼 on the Drawing toolbar**
    The Clip Art task pane opens. Each clip in the Clip Organizer is identified by descriptive keywords. At the top of the task pane in the Search for text box, you enter a keyword to search for clips that meet that description. You can search for a clip in a specific collection or in all collections. You can search for a clip that is a specific media type, such as clip art, photographs, movies, or sounds. At the bottom of the task pane, you can click one of the hyperlinks to organize clips, locate other pieces of clip art at the Office Online Web site, or read tips on how to find clip art.

3.  **Select any text in the Search for text box, type plans, then click Go**
    PowerPoint searches for clips identified by the keyword "plans".

> **QUICK TIP**
> Apply any of the "content" slide layouts except the Blank layout, then click the Insert Clip Art button in the Content placeholder to insert a piece of clip art.

4.  **Scroll down in the Clip Art task pane, then click the clip art thumbnail shown in Figure D-1**
    The clip art object appears in the center of the slide and the Picture toolbar opens. If you don't have the clip art picture shown in Figure D-1 in your Clip Organizer, select a similar picture.

5.  **Place the pointer over the lower-right sizing handle, then drag the handle down and to the right about ½"**
    The clip art object proportionally increases in size.

6.  **Click the Line Style button ☰ on the Picture toolbar, then click the 6pt solid line style**
    The clip art now has a 6-point border. It appears to be framed.

> **QUICK TIP**
> You can also use the keyboard arrow keys or the Nudge command on the Draw menu button to reposition any selected object by small increments.

7.  **Drag the clip art object to the right of the text object as shown in Figure D-2**
    The new clip art object appears next to the text object. Compare your screen to Figure D-2.

8.  **Click a blank area of the slide, then click the Save button 💾 on the Standard toolbar to save your changes**

**FIGURE D-1:** Screen showing Clip Art task pane

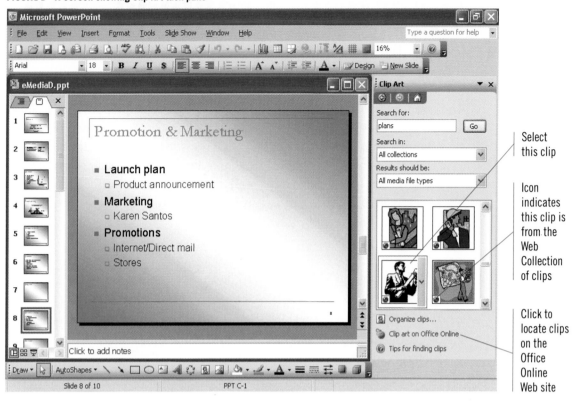

Select this clip

Icon indicates this clip is from the Web Collection of clips

Click to locate clips on the Office Online Web site

**FIGURE D-2:** Slide with clip art object resized and repositioned

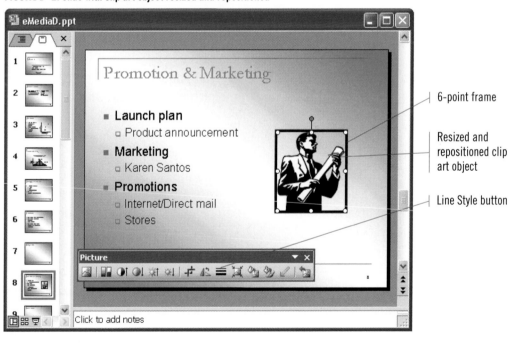

6-point frame

Resized and repositioned clip art object

Line Style button

PowerPoint 2003

## Clues to Use

### Find more clips online

If you can't find the clips you need in the Clip Organizer, you can easily download and use clips from the Clip Art and Media Web page in the Microsoft Office Online Web site. To get clips from the Clip Art and Media Web page, click the Clip art on Office Online hyperlink at the bottom of the Clip Art task pane. This will launch your Web browser and automatically connect you to the Microsoft Office Online Web site. You can search the site by keyword or browse by media type category. Each clip you download is automatically inserted into the Clip Organizer Web Collections folder and appears in the Clip Art task pane.

# Inserting, Cropping, and Scaling a Picture

A picture in PowerPoint is a scanned photograph, a piece of line art, clip art, or other artwork that is created in another program and inserted into a PowerPoint presentation. You can insert 18 types of pictures. As with other PowerPoint objects, you can move or resize an inserted picture. You can also crop pictures. **Cropping** a picture means to hide a portion of the picture. Although you can easily change a picture's size by drag-ging a corner sizing handle, you can also **scale** it to change its size by a specific percentage. In this lesson, you insert a picture that has previously been saved to a file, and then you crop and scale it and adjust its background.

## STEPS

**QUICK TIP**

You can also insert a picture by clicking the Insert Picture button on any of the Content slide layout placeholders.

1. **Click Slide 6 in the Slides tab, then click the Insert Picture button 🖼 on the Drawing toolbar**

   The Insert Picture dialog box opens. By default, the My Pictures folder is selected.

2. **Select the file PPT D-2.bmp from the drive and folder where your Data Files are stored, then click Insert**

   The picture appears in the center of the slide, and the Picture toolbar opens.

3. **Drag the picture to the right of the text object**

   The picture would fit better on the slide if it didn't show the boxes on the left side of the picture.

**TROUBLE**

If the Picture toolbar is in the way, drag it by its title bar.

4. **Click the Crop button ✛ on the Picture toolbar, then place the pointer over the left-middle sizing handle of the picture**

   The pointer changes to ⊣. When the Crop button is active, the sizing handles appear as straight black lines.

5. **Press and hold [Alt], then drag the left edge of the picture to the right until the dotted line indicating the left edge of the picture has cut out the boxes, as shown in Figure D-3, then click ✛**

   Pressing [Alt] while dragging or drawing an object in PowerPoint overrides the automatic snap-to-grid setting. Now the picture needs to be enlarged and positioned into place.

6. **Click the Format Picture button 🖌 on the Picture toolbar, click the Size tab in the Format Picture dialog box, make sure the Lock aspect ratio check box has a check mark, click the Height up arrow in the Scale section until the Height and Width percentages reach 175%, then click OK**

   When you are scaling a picture and Lock aspect ratio is selected, the ratio of height to width remains the same. The white background is distracting.

**QUICK TIP**

You cannot change the colors in a bit-mapped (.bmp) object in PowerPoint, but you can change the background col-ors of the object.

7. **With the picture still selected, click the Set Transparent Color button 🖋 on the Picture toolbar, the pointer changes to ✎, then click the white background in the picture**

   The white background is no longer visible, and the picture contrasts well with the background.

8. **Drag the picture to center it in the blank area to the right of the text object on the slide, click a blank area on the slide to deselect it, then save your changes**

   See Figure D-4.

**FIGURE D-3:** Using the cropping pointer to crop a picture

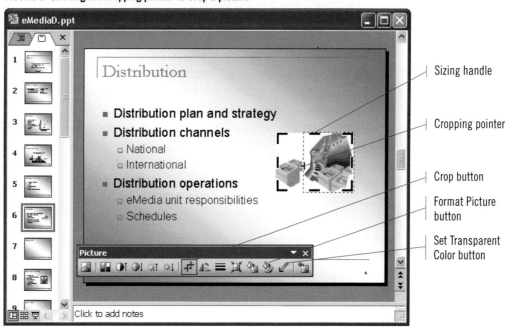

- Sizing handle
- Cropping pointer
- Crop button
- Format Picture button
- Set Transparent Color button

**FIGURE D-4:** Cropped and resized picture

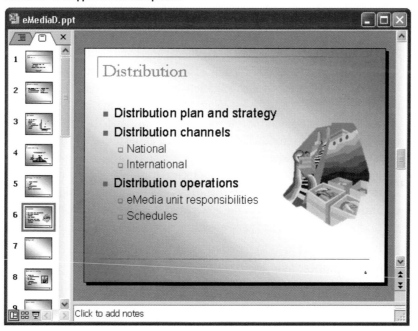

## Clues to Use

### Using graphics in PowerPoint

You can insert pictures with a variety of graphics file **formats**, or file types, in PowerPoint. Most of the clip art that comes with PowerPoint is in Windows metafile format and has the .wmf file extension. You can change the colors in a .wmf graphic object by selecting it, then clicking the Recolor Picture button 🖼 on the Picture toolbar. You can then replace each color in the graphic with another color. A graphic in .wmf format can be ungrouped into its separate PowerPoint objects, then edited with any of the PowerPoint drawing tools. You cannot recolor or ungroup pictures (files with the .bmp or .tif extension). The clip art you inserted in the last lesson is in .wmf format, and the picture you inserted in this lesson is in .bmp format.

You can also save PowerPoint slides as graphics and later use them in other presentations, in graphics programs, and on Web pages. Display the slide you want to save, then click Save As from the File menu. In the Save As dialog box, click the Save as type list arrow, and scroll to the desired graphics format. Name the file, click OK, then click the desired option when the alert box appears asking if you want to save all the slides or only the current slide.

# Embedding a Chart

Often, the best way to communicate information is with a visual aid such as a chart. PowerPoint comes with a program called **Microsoft Graph** that you can use to create charts for your slides. A **chart** is the graphical representation of numerical data. Every chart has a corresponding **datasheet** that contains the numerical data displayed by the chart. Table D-1 lists the chart types available in Microsoft Graph. When you insert a chart object into PowerPoint, you are actually embedding it. **Embedding** an object means that the object becomes part of the PowerPoint file, but you can double-click on the embedded object to display the tools of the program in which the object was created. If you modify the embedded object, the original object file does not change. ▚▚▚▚ You embed a chart on Slide 9 that shows the potential revenue of the eMedia product.

**STEPS**

1. **Click Slide 9 in the Slides tab, click the Other Task Panes list arrow ▼ on the task pane title bar, then click Slide Layout**

   The Slide Layout task pane opens with the Title and Text layout selected.

2. **Click the Title and Content layout thumbnail in the Content Layouts section of the Slide Layout task pane**

   Remember to use the ScreenTips to help locate the correct slide layout. A content placeholder appears on the slide. Six buttons are in the middle of the placeholder. Each of these buttons represents a different object, such as a table, picture, or chart, which you can apply to your slide.

   **QUICK TIP**
   You can also add a chart to a slide by clicking the Insert Chart button 📊 on the Standard toolbar.

3. **Click the Insert Chart button 📊 in the content placeholder**

   Microsoft Graph opens and embeds a default datasheet and chart into the slide, as shown in Figure D-5. The datasheet consists of rows and columns. The intersection of a row and a column is called a **cell**. Cells are referred to by their row and column location; for example, the cell at the intersection of column A and row 1 is called cell A1. Cells along the left column and top row of the datasheet typically contain **data labels** that identify the data in a column or row; for example, "East" and "1st Qtr" are data labels. Cells below and to the right of the data labels contain the data values that are represented in the chart. Each column and row of data in the datasheet is called a **data series**. Each data series has corresponding **data series markers** in the chart, which are graphical representations such as bars, columns, or pie wedges. The gray boxes along the left side of the datasheet are called **row headings** and the gray boxes along the top of the datasheet are called **column headings**. Notice that the PowerPoint Standard and Formatting toolbars have been replaced with the Microsoft Graph Standard and Formatting toolbars, and the menu bar has changed to include Microsoft Graph commands.

   **QUICK TIP**
   When Data and Chart are on the menu bar, you are working in Graph. Click outside the chart object to return to PowerPoint.

4. **Move the pointer over the datasheet**

   The pointer changes to ✚. Cell A1 is the **active cell**, which means that it is selected. The active cell has a thick black border around it.

5. **Click cell B3, which contains the value 46.9**

   Cell B3 is now the active cell.

6. **Click a blank area on the slide to exit Graph, then click again to deselect the chart object**

   The chart closes and the PowerPoint menu bar and toolbars appear.

7. **Save your changes**

Graph menu bar

Graph Standard and Formatting toolbars on one row

Row heading

Data label

Active cell

Data label

Column heading

Data series markers correspond to data series

Sales Outlook

|  | | A | B | C | D | E |
|---|---|---|---|---|---|---|
|  | | 1st Qtr | 2nd Qtr | 3rd Qtr | 4th Qtr | |
| 1 | East | 20.4 | 27.4 | 90 | 20.4 | |
| 2 | West | 30.6 | 38.6 | 34.6 | 31.6 | |
| 3 | North | 45.9 | 46.9 | 45 | 43.9 | |

Default datasheet

TABLE D-1: Microsoft Graph chart types

| chart type | looks like | use to |
|---|---|---|
| Column | | Track values over time or across categories |
| Bar | | Compare values in categories or over time |
| Line | | Track values over time |
| Pie | | Compare individual values to the whole |
| XY (Scatter) | | Compare pairs of values |
| Area | | Show contribution of each data series to the total over time |
| Doughnut | | Compare individual values to the whole with multiple series |
| Radar | | Show changes in values in relation to a center point |
| Surface | | Show value trends across two dimensions |
| Bubble | | Indicate relative size of data points |
| Stock | | Show stock market information or scientific data |
| Cylinder | | |
| Cone | | Track values over time or across categories |
| Pyramid | | |

PowerPoint 2003

# Entering and Editing Data in the Datasheet

After you embed the default chart into your presentation, you need to replace the data labels and numeric data with the correct information. If you have data in a spreadsheet or other source, you can import it into Microsoft Graph; otherwise you can type your own information into the datasheet. As you enter data in the cells or make changes to data labels in the datasheet, the chart automatically changes to reflect the new entries. ▄▄▄▄ You have been asked to create a chart showing the projected revenue figures for the first year of eMedia operation.

## STEPS

1. **Double-click the chart on Slide 9, then, if necessary, drag the Datasheet title bar to move the datasheet to the upper-right corner of the Slide pane**

   The chart is selected and the datasheet opens. The column data labels representing the quarters are correct, but the row data labels need adjusting, and the numeric data needs to be replaced with eMedia's projected quarterly sales figures for the Media and Publishing divisions.

2. **Click the East row label, type Media, then press [Enter]**

   After you press [Enter], the data label in Row 2 becomes selected. Pressing [Enter] in the datasheet moves the active cell down one cell; pressing [Tab] in the datasheet moves the active cell to the right one cell.

3. **Type Publish, then press [Tab]**

   Cell A2 becomes active. Notice in the chart, behind the datasheet, that the data labels you typed are now in the legend to the right of the chart. The information in Row 3 of the datasheet is not needed.

4. **Click the row heading for Row 3, then press [Delete]**

   Clicking the row heading for Row 3 selects the entire row. The default information in Row 3 of the datasheet is deleted and the columns in the chart adjust accordingly. The quarters appear along the horizontal axis, the values appear along the vertical axis in the chart.

5. **Click cell A1, type 17,000, press [Enter], type 14,500, press [Tab], then press [▲] to move to cell B1**

   Notice that the height of each column in the chart, as well as the values along the vertical axis, adjust to reflect the numbers you typed. The vertical axis is also called the **Value axis**. The horizontal axis is called the **Category axis**.

6. **Enter the rest of the numbers shown in Figure D-6 to complete the datasheet, then press [Enter]**

   The chart currently shows the columns grouped by quarter, and the legend represents the rows in the datasheet. The icons in the row headings indicate that the row labels appear in the legend. It would be more effective if the column data appeared in the legend so you could compare quarterly earnings for each eMedia product.

7. **Click the By Column button ▥ on the Standard toolbar**

   The division labels are now on the Category axis of the chart, and the quarters are listed in the legend. The groups of data markers (the columns) now represent the projected revenue for each product by quarter. Notice that the small column chart icons that used to be in the row headings in the datasheet have now moved to the column headings, indicating that the series are now in columns.

8. **Click a blank area on the slide, click again to deselect the chart object, compare your chart to Figure D-7, then save the presentation**

   The datasheet closes, allowing you to see your entire chart. This chart layout clearly shows eMedia's projected revenue for the first year it's in operation.

**FIGURE D-6:** Datasheet showing eMedia's projected revenue

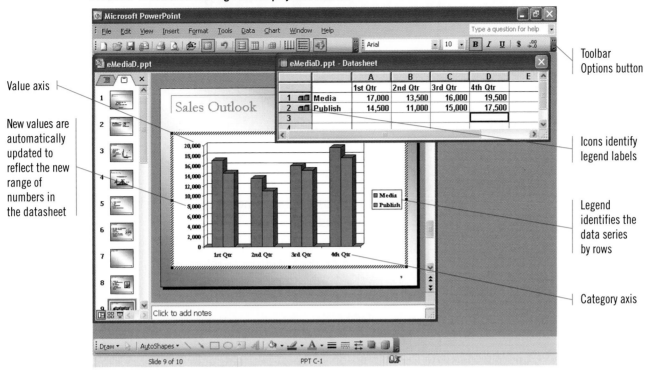

Value axis

New values are automatically updated to reflect the new range of numbers in the datasheet

Toolbar Options button

Icons identify legend labels

Legend identifies the data series by rows

Category axis

**FIGURE D-7:** Chart showing data grouped by division

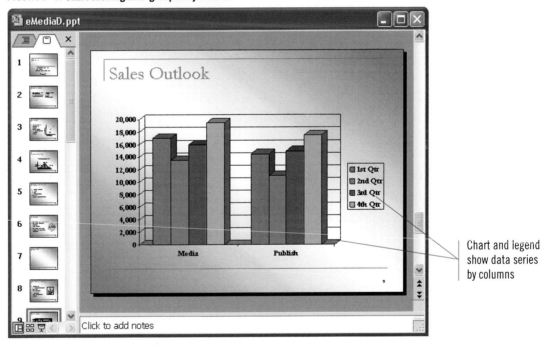

Chart and legend show data series by columns

## Clues to Use

### Series in Rows vs. Series in Columns

If you have difficulty visualizing the difference between the Series in Rows and the Series in Columns commands on the Data menu, think about what is represented in the legend. **Series in Rows** means that the information in the datasheet rows will be on the Value or vertical axis and is the information shown in the legend, and the column labels will be on the Category or horizontal axis.

**Series in Columns** means that the information in the columns becomes the information shown on the Value axis and in the legend, and the row labels will be on the horizontal or Category axis. Microsoft Graph places a small chart icon representing the chart type on the axis items that are currently represented by the chart series items, for example, bars, columns, or lines.

ENHANCING A PRESENTATION **POWERPOINT D-9**

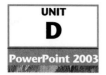

# Formatting a Chart

Microsoft Graph lets you change the appearance of the chart to emphasize certain aspects of the information you are presenting. You can change the chart type (for example pie, column, bar, or line), create titles, format the chart labels, move the legend, add arrows, or format the data series markers. Like other objects in PowerPoint, you can change the fill color, pattern, line style and color, and style of most elements in a chart. ▰▰▰▰ You want to improve the appearance of your chart by formatting the Value and Category axes and by inserting a title.

## STEPS

1. **Double-click the chart to open Microsoft Graph, then click the Close button ☒ in the Datasheet window to close the datasheet**

   The Microsoft Graph menu and toolbars remain at the top of the window.

2. **Click one of the revenue numbers on the Value axis to select the axis, then click the Currency Style button ⑤ on the Formatting toolbar**

   Before you can format any object on the chart, you need to select it. The numbers on the Value axis appear with dollar signs and two decimal places. You don't need to show the two decimal places because all the values are whole numbers.

3. **Click the Decrease Decimal button ⑭ on the Formatting toolbar twice**

   The numbers on the Value axis now have dollar signs and show only whole numbers. See Figure D-8. The division names on the Category axis would be easier to see if they were larger.

4. **Click one of the division names on the Category axis, click the Font Size list arrow ⑱ ▾ on the Formatting toolbar, then click 20**

   The font size changes from 18 points to 20 points for both labels on the Category axis. The chart would be easier to read if it had a title and axis labels.

5. **Click Chart on the menu bar, click Chart Options, then click the Titles tab, if it is not already selected**

   The Chart Options dialog box opens. You can change the chart title, axes, gridlines, legend, data labels, and the data table.

6. **Click in the Chart title text box, then type eMedia Projected Revenue**

   The preview box shows you how the chart looks with the title.

7. **Press [Tab] twice to move the insertion point to the Value (Z) axis text box, then type Revenue**

   In a 3-D chart, the Value axis is called the Z-axis, and the depth axis, which you don't usually work with, is the Y-axis. You decide to move the legend to the bottom of the chart.

8. **Click the Legend tab, click the Bottom option button, then click OK**

   The legend moves to the bottom of the chart, and the new chart title and axis title appear on the chart. The axis title would look better and take up less space if it were rotated 90 degrees.

9. **Right-click the Revenue label on the Value axis, click Format Axis Title, click the Alignment tab, drag the red diamond in the Orientation section counterclockwise to a vertical position so that the spin box reads 90 degrees, click OK, then click a blank area of the slide**

   Graph closes and the PowerPoint toolbars and menu bar appear.

10. **Drag the chart to the center of the slide, click a blank area of the slide, then save your changes**

    Compare your screen to Figure D-9.

**FIGURE D-8:** Chart showing applied Currency style to data

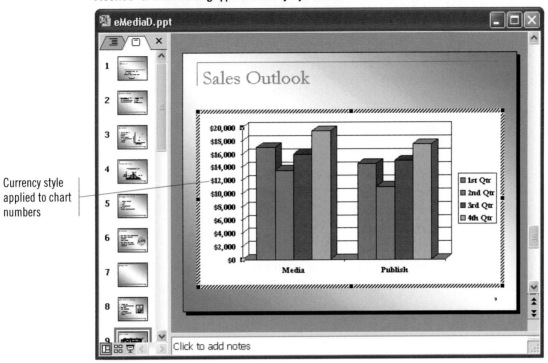

Currency style applied to chart numbers

**FIGURE D-9:** Slide showing formatted chart

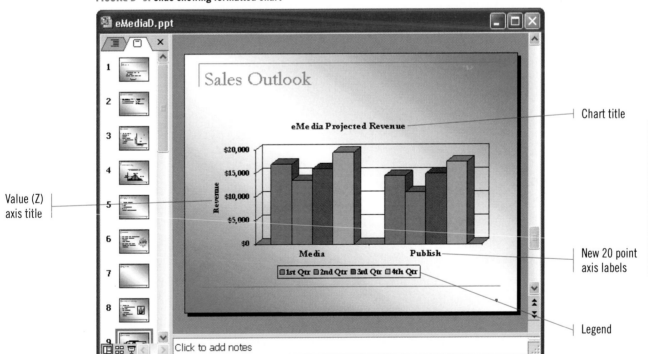

Value (Z) axis title

Chart title

New 20 point axis labels

Legend

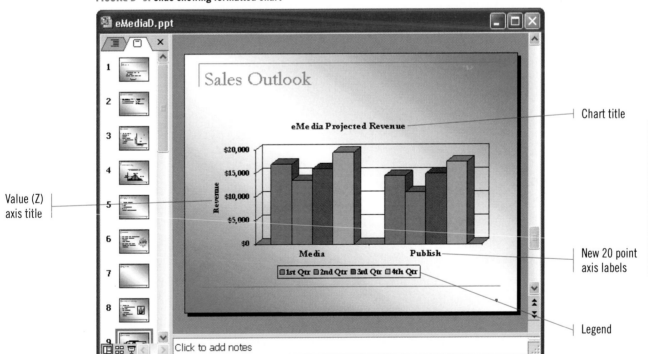

PowerPoint 2003

## Clues to Use

### Customizing data series in charts

You can easily customize the look of any chart in Microsoft Graph. Click the chart to select it, then double-click any data series element (a column, for example) to open the Format Data Series dialog box. Use the tabs to change the element's fill color, border, shape, or data label. You can even use the same fill effects you apply to a presentation background. In 3-D charts, you can change the chart depth as well as the distances between series.

# Creating Tables in PowerPoint

As you create your PowerPoint presentation, you may need to organize information into rows and columns. A table is ideal for this type of information. There are three ways to create a table in PowerPoint, you can click the Insert Table button on the Standard toolbar, the Table command on the Insert menu, or the Table icon on any of the content slide layouts. Once you have created a table, you can use the buttons on the Tables and Borders toolbar or on the Formatting toolbar to format the table to best present the information. █████ You decide to create a table describing eMedia's different pricing plans.

## STEPS

1. **Click Slide 7 in the Slides tab, then click the Insert Table button ▦ on the Standard toolbar**
   A grid appears that allows you to specify the number of columns and rows you want in your table.

**TROUBLE**

If the Tables and Borders toolbar does not open, click View on the menu bar, point to Toolbars, then click Tables and Borders. If the toolbar obscures part of the table, drag it out of the way.

2. **Move your pointer over the grid to select a 3 × 3 cell area ("3 × 3 Table" appears at the bottom of the grid), then click your mouse button**
   A table with three columns and three rows appears on the slide, and the Tables and Borders toolbar opens. The table has nine cells. The first cell in the table is selected and ready to accept text.

3. **Type Basic, press [Tab], type Standard, press [Tab], type Premium, then press [Tab]**
   The text you typed appears in the top three cells of the table. Pressing [Tab] moves the insertion point to the next cell. Pressing [Enter] moves the insertion point to the next line in the cell.

4. **Enter the rest of the table information shown in Figure D-10, do not press [Tab] after the last entry**
   Pressing [Tab] when the insertion point is in the cell in the last column and last row in a table creates a new row and places the insertion point in the cell in the first column of that row. The table would look better if it were formatted.

5. **Drag to select the entries in the top row of the table**
   The text in the first row becomes highlighted.

**QUICK TIP**

You can change the height or width of any table cell by dragging its top or side borders.

6. **Click the Center Vertically button ▤ on the Tables and Borders toolbar, then click the Center button ≡ on the Formatting toolbar**
   The text is centered horizontally and vertically.

7. **With the text in the first row still selected, click the Fill Color list arrow ▧ ▾ on the Tables and Borders toolbar, click the red color (Follow Title Text Scheme Color) in the first row, click the Font Color list arrow ▲ ▾ on the Formatting toolbar, click the white color (Follow Background Scheme Color) in the first row, then click a blank area of the slide**
   The cells in the top row are filled with the color red and the font color for the text in the cells is white.

8. **Select the text in the other two rows, vertically center the text, then fill these two rows with the white color (Follow Background Scheme Color) in the first row of the Fill Color list**
   The table would look better if the last two rows were a little farther away from the cell edges.

**QUICK TIP**

You can use the Format Table dialog box to apply a diagonal line through any table cell. Click the Borders tab, then click a diagonal line button.

9. **With the bottom two rows still selected, click Format on the menu bar, click Table, click the Text Box tab, click the Left up arrow until it reads .25, click OK, click a blank area of the slide, then save the presentation**
   The Tables and Borders toolbar closes and the table is no longer selected. Compare your screen with Figure D-11.

FIGURE D-10: The new table before formatting

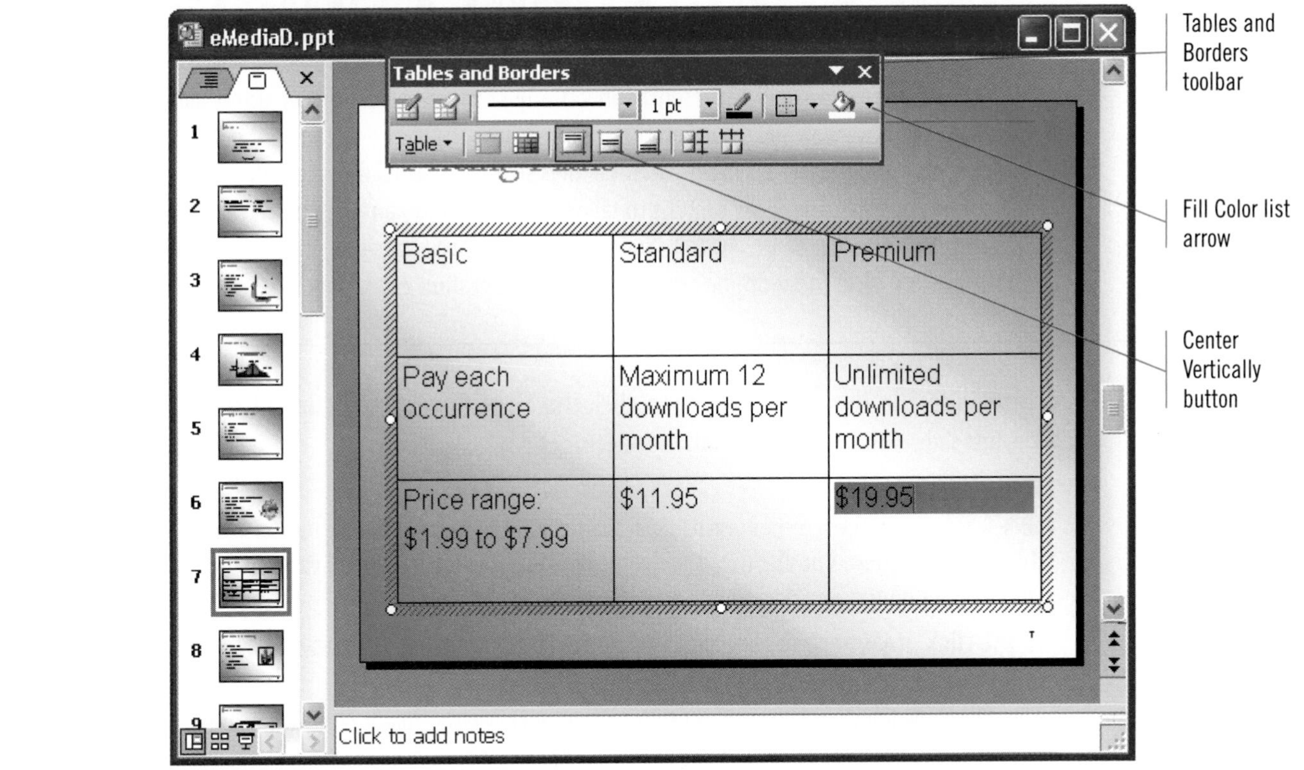

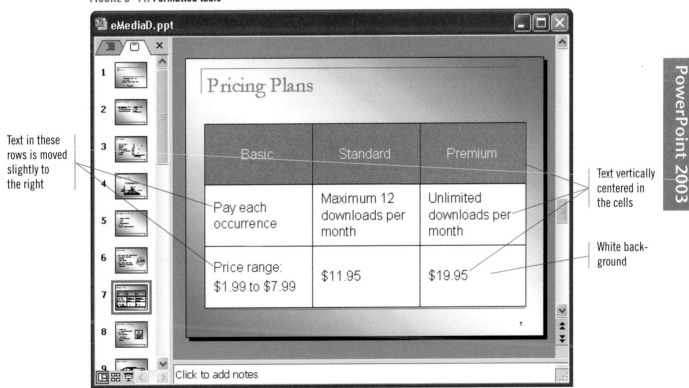

Tables and Borders toolbar

Fill Color list arrow

Center Vertically button

| Basic | Standard | Premium |
|---|---|---|
| Pay each occurrence | Maximum 12 downloads per month | Unlimited downloads per month |
| Price range: $1.99 to $7.99 | $11.95 | $19.95 |

FIGURE D-11: Formatted table

Text in these rows is moved slightly to the right

Text vertically centered in the cells

White background

## Pricing Plans

| Basic | Standard | Premium |
|---|---|---|
| Pay each occurrence | Maximum 12 downloads per month | Unlimited downloads per month |
| Price range: $1.99 to $7.99 | $11.95 | $19.95 |

# Using Slide Show Commands

With PowerPoint, you can show a presentation on any compatible computer using Slide Show view. As you've seen, Slide Show view fills your computer screen with the slides of your presentation, showing them one at a time, similarly to how a slide projector shows slides. Once your presentation is in Slide Show view, you can use a number of slide show options to tailor the show. For example, you can draw on, or **annotate**, slides or jump to a specific slide. ▓▓▓▓ You run the slide show of your presentation and practice using some of the custom slide show options to make your presentation more effective.

1. **Click** Slide 1 **in the Slides tab, then click the** Slide Show from current slide button ▯
   The first slide of the presentation fills the screen.

2. **Press** [Spacebar]
   Slide 2 appears on the screen. Pressing [Spacebar] or clicking the left mouse button is the easiest way to move through a slide show. Another way is to use the keys listed in Table D-2. You can also use the Slide Show short-cut menu for on-screen navigation during a slide show.

3. **Right-click anywhere on the screen, point to** Go to Slide **on the shortcut menu, then click** 6 Distribution
   The slide show jumps to Slide 6. You can highlight or emphasize major points in your presentation by anno-tating the slide during a slide show using one of PowerPoint's annotation tools.

> **QUICK TIP**
> The Slide Show menu buttons are transparent and will change to match the background color on the slide.

4. **Move the mouse across the screen to display the Slide Show toolbar, click the** Pen Options menu button ▱, **then click** Highlighter
   The pointer changes to ▮.

> **QUICK TIP**
> You have the option of saving annotations you create while in Slide Show view when you end or quit the slide show.

5. **Drag** ▮ **to highlight the words National, International, and Schedules**
   Compare your screen to Figure D-12. While the annotation tool is visible, mouse clicks do not advance the slide show; however, you can still move to the next slide by pressing [Spacebar] or [Enter].

6. **Click** ▱ **on the Slide Show toolbar, click** Erase All Ink on Slide, **then press** [Ctrl][A]
   The annotations on Slide 6 are erased and the pointer returns to ▯.

7. **Click the** Slide Show menu button ▭ **on the Slide Show toolbar, point to** Go to Slide, **then click** 9 Sales Outlook **on the menu**
   Slide 9 appears.

> **QUICK TIP**
> If you know the slide number of a slide you want to jump to during a slide show, type the number, then press [Enter].

8. **Press** [Home], **then click the left mouse button, press** [Spacebar], **or press** [Enter] **to advance through the slide show**
   After the black slide that indicates the end of the slide show appears, the next click ends the slide show and returns you to Normal view.

FIGURE D-12: Slide 6 in Slide Show view with highlight annotations

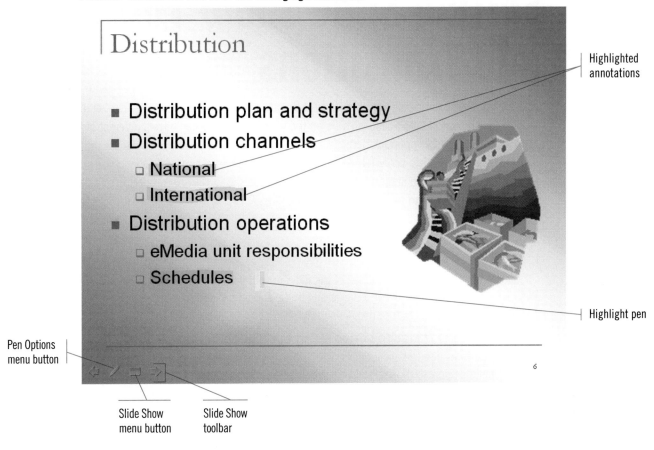

TABLE D-2: Basic Slide Show keyboard controls

| control | description |
| --- | --- |
| [Enter], [Spacebar], [PgDn], [N], [down arrow key], or [right arrow key] | Advances to the next slide |
| [E] | Erases the annotation drawing |
| [Home], [End] | Moves to the first or last slide in the slide show |
| [H] | Displays a hidden slide |
| [up arrow key] or [PgUp] | Returns to the previous slide |
| [W] | Changes the screen to white; press again to return |
| [S] | Pauses the slide show; press again to continue |
| [B] | Changes the screen to black; press again to return |
| [Ctrl][M] | Shows or hides annotations on the slide |
| [Ctrl][A] | Changes pointer to |
| [Esc] | Stops the slide show |

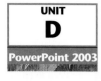
# Setting Slide Show Timings and Transitions

In a slide show, you can specify when and how each slide appears on the screen. You can set the **slide timing**, which is the amount of time a slide is visible on the screen. Each slide can have a different slide timing. Setting the right slide timing is important because it determines how long you have to discuss the material on each slide. You can also set **slide transitions**, which are the special visual and audio effects you apply to a slide that determine how it moves in and out of view during the slide show. ░░░░░You decide to set a 10 second slide timing for each slide and to set transitions for all the slides.

## STEPS

1. **Click the** Slide Sorter View button ▦

   Slide Sorter view shows a thumbnail of the slides in your presentation. The number of slides you see on your screen depends on the current zoom setting in the Zoom box on the Standard toolbar. Notice that the Slide Sorter toolbar appears next to the Standard toolbar.

   > **TROUBLE**
   > If you don't see ▦, click a Toolbar Options button ▾ on the Slide Sorter toolbar to locate buttons that are not visible on your toolbar.

2. **Click the** Slide Transition button ▦ **on the Slide Sorter toolbar**

   The Slide Transition task pane opens. The list box at the top of the task pane contains the slide transitions that you can apply to the slides of your presentation. Use the Modify transition section to change the speed of slide transitions. You can also add a sound to a slide so that it plays during a slide show. Use the Advance slide section to determine how slides progress during a slide show—either manually or with a slide timing.

3. **Make sure the** On mouse click check box **is selected in the Advance slide section, click the** Automatically after check box **to select it, drag to select the number in the Automatically after text box, type** 10, **then click** Apply to All Slides

   The timing between slides is 10 seconds which appears under each slide in Slide Sorter view. When you run the slide show, each slide will remain on the screen for 10 seconds. You can override a slide's timing and speed up the slide show by pressing [Spacebar], [Enter], or clicking the left mouse button.

   > **QUICK TIP**
   > Click the transition icon under any slide to see its transition play.

4. **Scroll down the list of transitions at the top of the task pane, click** Wheel Clockwise, 8 Spokes, **then click** Apply to All Slides

   All of the slides now have the Wheel Clockwise transition applied to them as indicated by the transition icon under each slide. You can apply a transition to one slide or to all of the slides in your presentation. The selected slide, Slide 1, displays the slide transition immediately after you apply the transition to all the slides. See Figure D-13. The slide transition would have more impact if it were slowed down.

5. **Click the** Speed list arrow **in the Modify transition section in the task pane, click** Medium, **then click** Apply to All Slides

6. **Scroll down the Slide Sorter view pane, click** Slide 10, **click the** Sound list arrow **in the Modify transition section in the task pane, scroll down the list, then click** Chime

   The sound plays when you apply the sound to the slide. The sound will now play when Slide 10 appears during the slide show.

   > **QUICK TIP**
   > To end a slide show, press [Esc] or click End Show on the Slide Show menu.

7. **Press** [Home], **click the** Slide Show button **in the Slide Transition task pane, then watch the slide show advance automatically**

8. **When you hear the chime and see the black slide at the end of the slide show, press** [Spacebar]

   The slide show ends and returns to Slide Sorter view with Slide 1 selected.

**FIGURE D-13:** Screen showing Slide Transition task pane

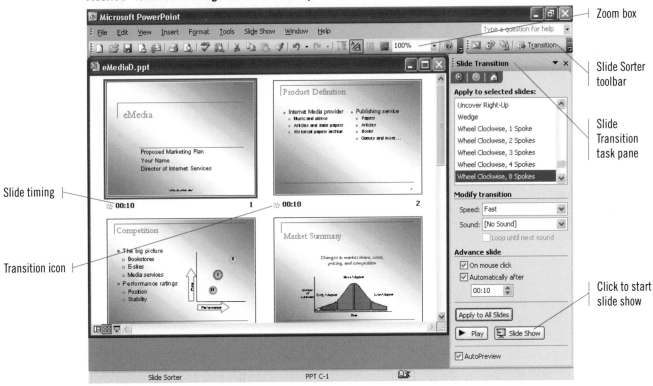

Zoom box

Slide Sorter toolbar

Slide Transition task pane

Slide timing

Transition icon

Click to start slide show

## Clues to Use

### Rehearsing slide show timing

You can set different slide timings for each slide. For example, you can have the title slide appear for 20 seconds, the second slide for 3 minutes, and so on. You can set timings by clicking the Rehearse Timings button on the Slide Sorter toolbar or by choosing the Rehearse Timings command on the Slide Show menu. The Rehearsal toolbar shown in Figure D-14 opens. It contains buttons to pause between slides and to advance to the next slide. After opening the Rehearsal toolbar, practice giving your presentation. PowerPoint keeps track of how long each slide appears and sets the timing accordingly. You can view your rehearsed timings in Slide Sorter view. The next time you run the slide show, you can use the timings you rehearsed.

**FIGURE D-14:** Rehearsal toolbar

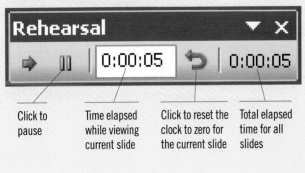

Click to pause

Time elapsed while viewing current slide

Click to reset the clock to zero for the current slide

Total elapsed time for all slides

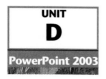

# Setting Slide Animation Effects

Animation effects let you control how the graphics and main points in your presentation appear on the screen during a slide show. You can animate text, images, or even individual chart elements, or you can add sound effects. You can set custom animation effects or use one of the PowerPoint animation schemes. An **animation scheme** is a set of predefined visual effects for the slide transition, title text, and bullet text of a slide. ▰▰▰ You want to animate the text and graphics of several slides in your presentation using PowerPoint animation schemes.

## STEPS

1. **In Slide Sorter view, click Slide 2, press and hold [Ctrl], click Slides 3, 5, 6, and 8, then release [Ctrl]**
   All of the selected slides have bulleted lists on them. The bullets can be animated to appear one at a time during a slide show.

2. **Click the Other Task Panes list arrow ▼, click Slide Design – Animation Schemes, scroll down the Apply to selected slides list to the Exciting section, then click Neutron**
   Each of the selected slides previews the Neutron animation scheme.

3. **Click Slide 1, click the Slide Show button on the Slide Design – Animation Schemes task pane, then press [Esc] when you see the black slide**
   The Neutron animation scheme is displayed on the selected slides. You can also animate objects on a slide by setting custom animations. To set custom animation effects, the slide you want to animate must be in Slide view.

4. **Double-click Slide 3 in Slide Sorter view, click Slide Show on the menu bar, then click Custom Animation**
   The Custom Animation task pane opens. Objects that are already animated appear in the Custom Animation task pane list in the order in which they will be animated. **Animation tags** on the slide label the order in which elements are animated during a slide show.

5. **Click the grouped arrow object on the slide to select it, then click the Add Effect button in the Custom Animation task pane**
   A menu of animation effects appears.

6. **Point to Entrance, then click More Effects**
   The Add Entrance Effect dialog box opens. All of the effects in this dialog box allow an object to enter the slide using a special effect.

7. **Scroll down to the Exciting section, click Pinwheel, then click OK**
   The arrow object now has the pinwheel effect applied to it as shown in Figure D-15.

8. **Run the Slide Show from Slide 1**
   The special effects make the presentation more interesting to view.

9. **Click the Slide Sorter View button ▦, click the Zoom list arrow on the Standard toolbar, then click 50%**
   Figure D-16 shows the completed presentation in Slide Sorter view at 50% zoom.

10. **Add your name as a footer on the notes and handouts, save your presentation, print it as handouts (6 slides per page), then close the presentation and exit PowerPoint**

> **QUICK TIP**
> Keep in mind that the animation effects you choose give a certain "flavor" to your presentation. They can be serious and business-like or humorous. Choose appropriate effects for your presentation content and audience.

> **QUICK TIP**
> If you want the parts of a grouped object to animate individually, then you must ungroup them first.

> **QUICK TIP**
> To change the order in which objects are animated on the slide, select the object you want to change in the Custom Animation list in the task pane, then click the appropriate Re-Order arrow below the list.

FIGURE D-15: Screen with Custom Animation task pane open

Animation tag

Animation tag for grouped arrow object

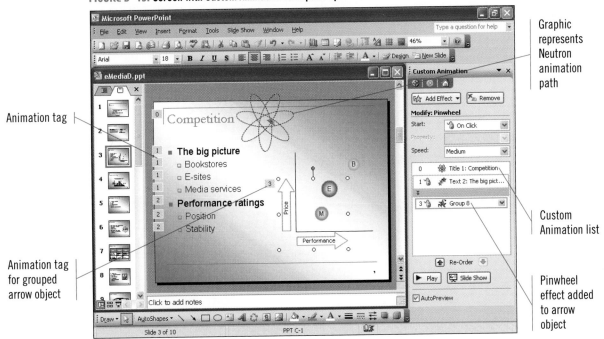

Graphic represents Neutron animation path

Custom Animation list

Pinwheel effect added to arrow object

FIGURE D-16: Completed presentation in Slide Sorter view

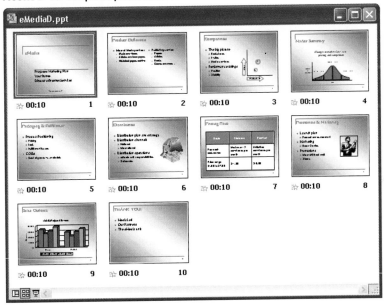

## Clues to Use

### Presentation checklist

You should always rehearse your slide show. If possible, rehearse your presentation in the room and with the computer that you will use. Use the following checklist to prepare for the slide show:

- Is **PowerPoint** or **PowerPoint Viewer** installed on the computer?
- Is your **presentation file** on the hard drive of the computer you will be using? Try putting a shortcut for the file on the desktop. Do you have a backup copy of your presentation file on a floppy disk?
- Is the **projection device** working correctly? Can the slides be seen from the back of the room?

- Do you know how to control **room lighting** so that the audience can see both your slides and their handouts and notes? You may want to designate someone to control the lights if the controls are not close to you.
- Will the **computer** be situated so you can advance and annotate the slides yourself? If not, designate someone to advance them for you.
- Do you have enough copies of your **handouts**? Bring extras. Decide when to hand them out, or whether you prefer to have them waiting at the audience members' seats when they enter.

# Practice

## ▼ CONCEPTS REVIEW

**Label each element of the PowerPoint window shown in Figure D-17.**

FIGURE D-17

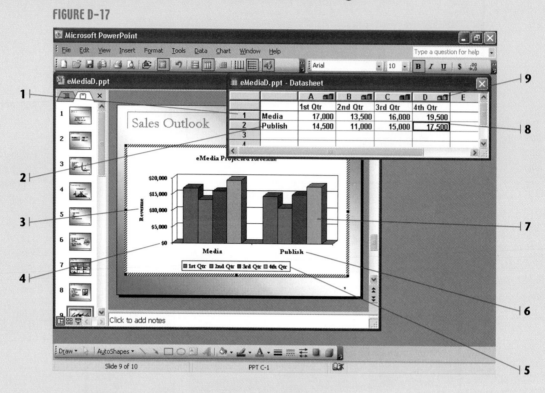

**Match each term with the statement that best describes it.**

10. Annotate
11. Data series markers
12. Crop
13. Datasheet
14. Chart
15. Animation scheme

a. Graphical representations of numerical data
b. A set of predefined visual effects
c. A graphical representation of numerical data
d. Where the numerical data is stored for a chart
e. To hide a portion of a picture
f. To draw on a slide during a slide show

**Select the best answer from the list of choices.**

16. **When you want an object to become a part of a PowerPoint file you:**
   a. Annotate the object.
   b. Embed the object.
   c. Crop the object.
   d. Scale the object.

17. **Professionally designed images that you can place in your presentation are called:**
   a. Thumbnails.
   b. Pictures.
   c. Clip art.
   d. AutoShapes.

18. **Cropping is essentially the same as:**
   a. Hiding.
   b. Deleting.
   c. Resizing.
   d. Scaling.

19. **What are you doing when you drag a sizing handle of an object?**
   a. Moving
   b. Scaling
   c. Hiding
   d. Deleting

**20. What does pressing [Alt] while dragging an object's sizing handle do?**

    **a.** Overrides the automatic snap-to-grid setting      **c.** Deletes that portion of the object

    **b.** Constrains the proportions of the object      **d.** Scales the object larger or smaller

**21. What is a chart in PowerPoint?**

    **a.** A datasheet that contains numerical data      **c.** A graphical representation of numerical data

    **b.** A table you create with the Diagram button      **d.** An organizational chart

**22. Where is the numerical data for a chart found?**

    **a.** The data series markers      **c.** The chart

    **b.** The slide      **d.** The datasheet

**23. Which axis is the vertical axis?**

    **a.** Value axis      **c.** Legend axis

    **b.** Category axis      **d.** Horizontal axis

# ▼ SKILLS REVIEW

**1. Insert clip art.**

    **a.** Open the presentation PPT D-3.ppt from the drive and folder where your Data Files are stored, then save it as **Year End Report**.

    **b.** Go to Slide 2, search for clip art using the keyword CD, then insert the clip on the slide.

    **c.** On the Picture tab of the Format Picture dialog box, click the Color list arrow, then click Grayscale.

    **d.** Drag the graphic so the top of the graphic aligns with the body text box and is centered in the blank area on the right of the slide, then save your changes.

**2. Insert, crop, and scale a picture.**

    **a.** Go to Slide 6 and insert the picture file PPT D-4.jpg.

    **b.** Crop about ¾" off the top of the picture.

    **c.** Drag the picture so its top is aligned with the top line of text.

    **d.** Scale the picture to 65%, then using the Color button on the picture toolbar change the picture to grayscale.

    **e.** Reposition the graphic, then save your changes.

**3. Embed a chart.**

    **a.** Go to Slide 3, 2005 CD Sales by Quarter, and apply the Title and Content layout.

    **b.** Start Microsoft Graph.

    **c.** Deselect the chart object and save your changes.

**4. Enter and edit data in the datasheet.**

    **a.** Open Graph again.

    **b.** Enter the information shown in Table D-4 into the datasheet.

    **c.** Delete any unused rows of default data.

    **d.** Place the data series in columns.

    **e.** Save your changes.

**TABLE D-4**

| | 1st Qtr | 2nd Qtr | 3rd Qtr | 4th Qtr |
|---|---|---|---|---|
| East Div. | 405 | 340 | 390 | 320 |
| West Div. | 280 | 320 | 380 | 250 |

**5. Format a chart.**

    **a.** Close the datasheet but leave Graph running.

    **b.** Change the region names font on the Category axis to 20 point and regular font style (no bold).

    **c.** Apply the Currency Style with no decimals to the values on the Value axis.

    **d.** Insert the chart title **Division Sales**.

    **e.** Add the title **Thousands** to the Value axis, then change the alignment of this label to vertical.

    **f.** Change the legend text font to 16-point Arial font and regular font style (no bold).

    **g.** Exit Graph and save your changes.

**6. Create a table.**

    **a.** Insert a new slide after Slide 2 using the Title and Content slide layout.

    **b.** Add the slide title **CD Sales by Type**.

    **c.** Click the Insert Table button in the placeholder, then insert a table with two columns and five rows.

    **d.** Enter **Type** in the first cell and **Sales** in the second cell in the first row.

    **e.** In the first column, enter the following: **Rock**, **Rap**, **New Age**, and **Country**.

**f.** In the second column, enter sales figures: **20,000**, **35,000**, **55,650**, and **80,000** for each CD type.

**g.** Format the table using fills, horizontal and vertical alignment, and other features.

**h.** Save your changes.

### 7. Use slide show commands.

**a.** Begin the slide show at Slide 1, then proceed through the slide show to Slide 3.

**b.** On Slide 3, use the Ballpoint pen to draw straight-line annotations under each type of music.

**c.** Erase the pen annotations, then change the pointer back to an arrow.

**d.** Go to 5 Summary slide using the Slide Show menu button on the Slide Show toolbar, then using the Highlighter, highlight all of the points on the slide.

**e.** Press [End] to move to the last slide. Don't save any changes.

**f.** Return to Normal view.

### 8. Set slide show timings and transitions.

**a.** Switch to Slide Sorter view, then open the Slide Transition task pane.

**b.** Specify that all slides should advance after eight seconds.

**c.** Apply the Newsflash transition effect to all slides.

**d.** View the slide show to verify the transitions are correct, then save your changes.

### 9. Set slide animation effects.

**a.** Switch to Normal view, then open the Custom Animation task pane.

**b.** Switch to Slide 5, apply the (Entrance) Fly In animation effect to the bulleted list.

**c.** Go to Slide 2, apply the (Emphasis) Shimmer animation effect to the text object. (*Hint*: Look in the Moderate section after clicking More effects.)

**d.** Apply the (Exit) Faded Zoom animation effect to the graphic on Slide 2. (*Hint*: Look in the Subtle section after clicking More effects.)

**e.** Run the slide show from the beginning to check the animation effects.

**f.** Add your name as a footer to the notes and handouts, then print the presentation as handouts (4 slides per page).

**g.** Save your changes, close the presentation, and exit PowerPoint.

# ▼ INDEPENDENT CHALLENGE 1

You are a financial management consultant for Northwest Investments, located in Tacoma, Washington. One of your responsibilities is to create standardized presentations on different financial investments for use on the company Web site. In this challenge, you enhance the look of the slides by adding and formatting objects and adding animation effects and transitions.

**a.** Open the file PPT D-5.ppt from the drive and folder where your Data Files are stored, and save it as **Web Seminar1**.

**b.** Add your name as the footer on all slides and handouts.

**c.** Apply the Title and Chart layout to Slide 6, and enter the data in Table D-5 into the datasheet.

**d.** Format the chart. Add titles as necessary.

**TABLE D-5**

| | 1 year | 3 year | 5 year | 10 year |
|---|---|---|---|---|
| Bonds | 4.2% | 5.2% | 7.9% | 9.4% |
| Stocks | 4.5% | 6.3% | 9.8% | 10.6% |
| Mutual Funds | 6.1% | 6.3% | 7.4% | 8.1% |

**Advanced Challenge Exercise**

- Double-click one of the 10 year data series markers to select the data series.
- On the Data Labels tab, click the Series name check box.
- On the Patterns tab, click the red color in the Area section.

**e.** Add an appropriate clip art item to Slide 2, then format as necessary.

**f.** On Slide 4, use the Align and Group commands to organize the shapes.

**g.** Spell check the presentation, then save it.

**h.** View the slide show, evaluate your presentation, and add a template of your choice. Make changes if necessary.

**i.** Set animation effects, slide transitions, and slide timings, keeping in mind that your audience includes potential investors who need the information you are presenting to make decisions about where to put their hard-earned money.

**j.** View the slide show again.

**k.** Print the slides as handouts (6 slides per page), then close the presentation, and exit PowerPoint.

# ▼ INDEPENDENT CHALLENGE 2

You are the manager of the Indiana University Student Employment Office. Work-study students staff the office; new students start every semester. Create a presentation that you can use to train them.

   **a.** Plan and create the slide presentation. As you plan your outline, make sure you include slides that will help explain to the work-study staff the main features of the office, including its employment database, library of company directories, seminars on employment search strategies, interviewing techniques, and resume development, as well as its student consulting and resume bulk-mailing services. Add more slides with more content if you wish.

   **b.** Use an appropriate design template.

   **c.** Add clip art and photographs available in the Clip Organizer to help create visual interest.

   **d.** Save the presentation as **Indiana USEO** to the drive and folder where your Data Files are stored. View the slide show and evaluate the contents of your presentation. Make any necessary adjustments.

   **e.** Add transitions, special effects, and timings to the presentation. Remember that your audience is university students who need to assimilate a lot of information in order to perform well in their new jobs. View the slide show again to evaluate the effects you added.

   **f.** Add your name as a footer to slides and handouts. Spell check, save, and print the presentation as handouts (4 slides per page).

   **g.** Close the presentation and exit PowerPoint.

# ▼ INDEPENDENT CHALLENGE 3

You are the managing development engineer at SportDesign, Inc, an international sports product design company located in Ottawa, Ontario, Canada. SportDesign designs and manufactures items such as bike helmets, bike racks, and kayak paddles, and markets these items primarily to countries in North America and Western Europe. You need to create a quarterly presentation that outlines the progress of the company's newest technologies, and present it.

   **a.** Plan and create a slide show presentation that includes two new technologies.

   **b.** Use an appropriate design template.

   **c.** Add one chart and one table in the presentation that shows details (such as performance results, testing criteria, etc.) about the new technologies.

   **d.** Include at least two slides that explain how the new technologies will appeal specifically to individual countries in the European and North American markets.

   **e.** Set slide transitions, animation effects, and slide timings. View the slide show to evaluate the effects you added.

**Advanced Challenge Exercise**

   ■  Click the Rehearse Timings button on the Slide Sorter toolbar.

   ■  Set slide timings for each slide in the presentation.

   ■  Save new slide timings.

   **f.** Add your name as a footer to the handouts. Save the presentation as **SportDesign** to the drive and folder where your Data Files are stored.

   **g.** Print the presentation as handouts (4 slides per page), then close the presentation and exit PowerPoint.

 ▼ INDEPENDENT CHALLENGE 4

You work for IRAssets, a small retirement investment firm. You have been asked to complete a retirement investing presentation started by your boss. Most of the information has already been entered into the PowerPoint presentation; you just need to add a template and a table to complete the presentation. To find the data for the table, you need to use the Web to locate certain information.

You'll need to find the following information on the Web:

   •  Data for a table that compares the traditional IRA with the Roth IRA.

   •  Data for a table that compares at least two other retirement plans.

# ▼ INDEPENDENT CHALLENGE 4 (CONTINUED)

**a.** Open the file PPT D-6.ppt from the drive and folder where your Data Files are stored and save it as **Retirement**.

**b.** Connect to the Internet, then use a search engine to locate Web sites that have information on retirement plans.

**c.** Review at least two Web sites that contain information about retirement plans. Print the Home pages of the Web sites you use to gather data for your presentation.

**d.** Apply the Title and Table layout to Slide 7, then enter the data you found that compares the IRA retirement plans.

**e.** Apply the Title and Table layout to Slide 8, then enter the data you found that compares the other retirement plans.

**f.** Apply a template to the presentation, then customize the slide background and the color scheme.

**g.** Format the Autoshape objects on Slides 4 and 5.

**h.** Use text formatting to help emphasize important points, then add your name as a footer to the handouts.

**i.** Add slide transitions, slide timings, and animation effects.

**j.** Spell check the presentation, view the slide show, save the final version, then print the handouts.

**k.** Close the presentation and exit PowerPoint.

# ▼ VISUAL WORKSHOP

Create a slide with a chart that looks like the slide in Figure D-18. Add your name as a footer on the slide. Save the presentation as **2006 Expenses** to the drive and folder where your Data Files are stored.

**FIGURE D-18**

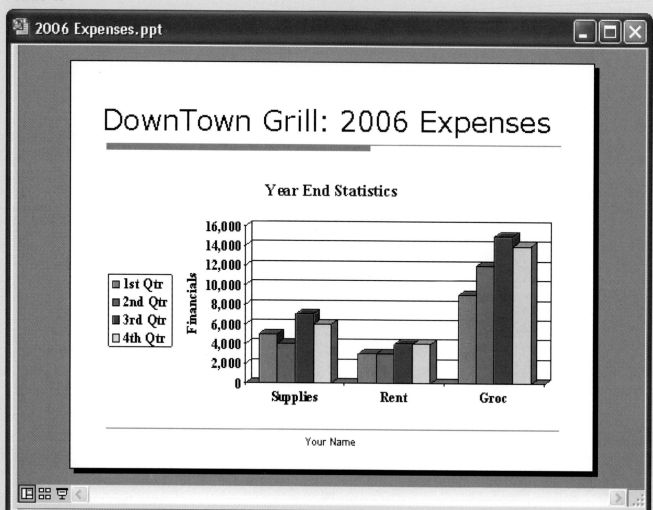

# Glossary

**Active cell** A selected cell in a Graph datasheet or an Excel worksheet.

**Adjustment handle** A small yellow diamond that changes the appearance of an object's most prominent feature.

**Align** To place objects' edges or centers on the same plane.

**Animation scheme** A set of predefined visual effects for a slide transition, title text, and bullet text of the slides in a PowerPoint presentation.

**Animation tag** Identifies the order in which objects are animated on a slide during a slide show.

**Annotate** A freehand drawing on the screen made by using the Annotation tool. You can annotate only in Slide Show view.

**AutoContent Wizard** A wizard that helps you get a presentation started by supplying a sample outline and a design template.

**.bmp** The abbreviation for the bitmap graphics file format.

**Background** The area behind the text and graphics on a slide.

**Body text** Subpoints or bullet points on a slide under the slide title.

**Body text placeholder** A reserved box on a slide for main points.

**Bullet** A small graphic symbol, usually a round or square dot, often used to identify items in a list.

**Category axis** The horizontal axis in a chart.

**Cell** The intersection of a column and row in a worksheet, datasheet, or table.

**Chart** A graphical representation of information from a datasheet or worksheet. Types include 2-D and 3-D column, bar, pie, area, and line charts.

**Clip art** Predesigned graphic images you can insert in any document or presentation to enhance its appearance.

**Clip Organizer** A library of art, pictures, sounds, video clips, and animations that all Office applications share.

**Color scheme** The set of eight coordinated colors that make up a PowerPoint presentation; a color scheme assigns colors for text, lines, objects, and background. You can change the color scheme on any presentation at any time.

**Column heading** Gray boxes along the top of a datasheet.

**Crop** To hide part of a picture or object using the Cropping tool.

**Data label** Information that identifies the data in a column or row in a datasheet.

**Data series** A column or row in a datasheet.

**Data series marker** A graphical representation of a data series, such as a bar or column.

**Datasheet** The component of a chart that contains the numerical data displayed in a chart.

**Design template** Predesigned slide design with formatting and color schemes that you can apply to an open presentation.

**Dialog box** A window that opens when a program needs more information to carry out a command.

**Drawing toolbar** A toolbar that contains buttons that let you create lines, shapes, and special effects.

**Embedded object** An object that is created in one application and copied to another. Embedded objects remain connected to the original program file in which they were created for easy editing.

**File** The presentation you create using PowerPoint.

**File format** A file type, such as .bmp, .jpg, or .gif.

**Filename** The name of a presentation file.

**Folder** A subdivision of a disk that works like a filing system to help you organize files.

**Formatting toolbar** A toolbar that contains buttons for the most frequently used formatting commands.

**G.gif** The abbreviation for the graphics interchange format file.

**Grid** Evenly spaced horizontal and vertical lines that appear on a slide when it is being created to help place objects. Lines do not appear when slide is shown or printed.

**Group** To combine multiple objects into one object.

**Insertion point** A blinking vertical line that indicates where the next character will appear when text is entered in a text placeholder in PowerPoint.

**Menu bar** The bar beneath the title bar that contains menus from which you choose program commands.

**Microsoft Graph** The program that creates a datasheet and chart to graphically depict numerical information.

**Normal view** A presentation view that divides the presentation window into three sections: Slides or Outline tab, Slide pane, and notes pane.

**Notes Page view** A presentation view that displays a reduced image of the current slide above a large text box where you can type notes.

**Notes pane** The area in Normal view that shows speaker notes for the current slide; also in Notes Page view, the area below the slide image that contains speaker notes.

**Object** An item you place or draw on a slide that can be manipulated. Objects are drawn lines and shapes, text, clip art, imported pictures, and embedded objects.

**Outline tab** The section in Normal view that displays your presentation text in the form of an outline, without graphics.

**Pane** A section of the PowerPoint window, such as the Slide or notes pane.

**Placeholder** A dashed line box where you place text or objects.

**PowerPoint Viewer** A special application designed to run a PowerPoint slide show on any compatible computer that does not have PowerPoint installed.

**PowerPoint window** A window that contains the running PowerPoint application. The PowerPoint window includes the PowerPoint menus, toolbars, and Presentation window.

**Presentation software** A software program used to organize and present information.

**Rotate handle** A green circular handle at the top of a selected object that you can drag to rotate the selected object upside-down, sideways, or to any angle in between.

**Row heading** The gray box containing the row number to the left of the row in a datasheet.

**Scale** To change the size of a graphic to a specific percentage of its original size.

**Scroll** To use the scroll bars or arrow keys to display different parts of a PowerPoint window.

**Selection box** A slanted line border that appears around a text object or placeholder, indicating that it is ready to accept text.

**Series in Columns** The information in the columns of a datasheet that are on the Value axis; the row labels are on the Category axis.

**Series in Rows** The information in the datasheet rows that are on the Value axis; the column labels are the Category axis.

**Sizing handles** The small circles that appear around a selected object. Dragging a handle resizes the object.

**Slide layout** This determines how all of the elements on a slide are arranged, including text and content placeholders.

**Slide pane** The section of Normal view that contains the current slide.

**Slide Show view** A view that shows a presentation as an electronic slide show; each slide fills the screen.

**Slide Sorter view** A view that displays a thumbnail of all slides in the order in which they appear in your presentation; used to rearrange slides and add special effects.

**Slide timing** The amount of time a slide is visible on the screen during a slide show.

**Slide transition** The special effect that moves one slide off the screen and the next slide on the screen during a slide show. Each slide can have its own transition effect.

**Slides tab** The section in Normal View that displays the slides of your presentation as small thumbnails.

**Standard toolbar** The toolbar containing the buttons that perform some of the most commonly used commands such as Cut, Copy, Paste, Save, Open, and Print.

**Status bar** The bar at the bottom of the PowerPoint window that contains messages about what you are doing and seeing in PowerPoint, such as the current slide number or a description of a command or button.

**Subtitle text placeholder** A box on the title slide reserved for subpoint text.

**Task pane** A separate pane available in all the PowerPoint views except Slide Show view that contains sets of menus, lists, options, and hyperlinks for commonly used commands.

**Text label** A text box you create using the Text Box button, where the text does not automatically wrap inside the box. Text box text does not appear in the Outline tab.

**Text box** Any text you create using the Text Box button. A word processing box and a text label are both examples of a text box.

**Text placeholder** A box with a dashed-line border and text that you replace with your own text.

**Thumbnail** A small image of a slide. Thumbnails are visible on the Slides tab and in Slide Sorter view.

**Timing** *See* Slide timing.

**Title** The first line or heading on a slide.

**Title bar** The bar at the top of the program window that indicates the program name and the name of the current file.

**Title placeholder** A box on a slide reserved for the title of a presentation or slide.

**Title slide** The first slide in a presentation.

**V**alue axis The vertical axis in a chart.

**View** A way of displaying a presentation, such as Normal view, Notes Page view, Slide Sorter view, and Slide Show view.

**View buttons** The buttons at the bottom of the Outline tab and the Slides tab that you click to switch among views.

**W**.wmf The abbreviation for the Windows metafile file format, which is the format of some clip art.

**Window** A rectangular area of the screen where you view and work on the open file.

**Wizard** An interactive set of dialog boxes that guides you through a task.

**Word processing box** A text box you create using the Text Box button, where the text automatically wraps inside the box.

# Index

## ►A

Add command, POWERPOINT B-15

Add words to command, POWERPOINT B-15

adjustment handle, POWERPOINT C-6, POWERPOINT C-7

aligning objects, POWERPOINT C-8, POWERPOINT C-9

All Programs menu, POWERPOINT A-4, POWERPOINT A-5

animation effects, POWERPOINT D-18–19

animation schemes, POWERPOINT D-18

annotations

   saving, POWERPOINT D-14

   Slide Show view, POWERPOINT D-14

area charts, POWERPOINT D-7

arrow keys, moving objects, POWERPOINT D-2

audience impact, POWERPOINT B-17

AutoContent Wizard, POWERPOINT A-8–9

AutoCorrect command, POWERPOINT B-15

AutoShapes, applying shaded background, POWERPOINT C-16

## ►B

Back button, Save As dialog box, POWERPOINT A-13

background

   colors, POWERPOINT D-4

   customizing, POWERPOINT C-16, POWERPOINT C-17

bar charts, POWERPOINT D-7

bitmapped objects, colors, POWERPOINT D-4

black and white, viewing presentations, POWERPOINT A-17

body text placeholders, POWERPOINT B-6, POWERPOINT B-7

bubble charts, POWERPOINT D-7

bulleted list placeholder, POWERPOINT B-7

buttons. See also specific buttons

   Slide Show menu, POWERPOINT D-14

## ►C

cells, tables. See table cells

Change/Change All command, POWERPOINT B-15

chart(s)

customizing data series, POWERPOINT D-11

   embedding, POWERPOINT D-6–7

   formatting, POWERPOINT D-10–11

   types, POWERPOINT D-7

chart placeholder, POWERPOINT B-7

checklist for presentations, POWERPOINT D-19

clip art

   cropping, POWERPOINT D-4, POWERPOINT D-5

   inserting, POWERPOINT D-2–3

   online sources, POWERPOINT D-3

   scaling, POWERPOINT D-4, POWERPOINT D-5

clip art placeholder, POWERPOINT B-7

closing files, POWERPOINT A-16, POWERPOINT A-17

color(s)

   background, POWERPOINT D-4

   bitmapped objects, POWERPOINT D-4

   printing files, POWERPOINT A-16

color schemes

   applying to selected slides, POWERPOINT C-16

   customizing, POWERPOINT C-16, POWERPOINT C-17

column charts, POWERPOINT D-7

column width, datasheets, POWERPOINT D-8

cone charts, POWERPOINT D-7

content placeholder, POWERPOINT B-7, POWERPOINT D-2

correcting errors, spelling, POWERPOINT B-14–15

Create New Folder button, Save As dialog box, POWERPOINT A-13

cropping clip art, POWERPOINT D-4, POWERPOINT D-5

customizing

   background, POWERPOINT C-16, POWERPOINT C-17

   color scheme, POWERPOINT C-16, POWERPOINT C-17

   data series in charts, POWERPOINT D-11

Cut button, POWERPOINT C-10

Cut command, POWERPOINT C-10

cylinder charts, POWERPOINT D-7

## D

**data series**, customizing, POWERPOINT D-11

**datasheets**, POWERPOINT D-6, POWERPOINT D-7

column width, POWERPOINT D-8

editing data, POWERPOINT D-8, POWERPOINT D-9

entering data, POWERPOINT D-8, POWERPOINT D-9

**dates, entering**, POWERPOINT B-10

**Delete button**, Save As dialog box, POWERPOINT A-13

**design templates**, POWERPOINT B-1, POWERPOINT B-12–13

**desktop**, creating shortcuts, POWERPOINT A-4

**diagram placeholder**, POWERPOINT B-7

**displaying rulers**, POWERPOINT C-6

**doughnut charts**, POWERPOINT D-7

**drawing objects**, POWERPOINT C-4, POWERPOINT C-5

**Drawing toolbar**, POWERPOINT A-6, POWERPOINT A-7

## E

**editing**

data in datasheets, POWERPOINT D-8, POWERPOINT D-9

drawn objects, POWERPOINT C-6–7

**embedding charts**, POWERPOINT D-6–7

**End Show button**, POWERPOINT D-14

**ending slide shows**, POWERPOINT D-14

**error correction**, spell checking, POWERPOINT B-14–15

**evaluating presentations**, POWERPOINT B-16–17

**exiting PowerPoint**, POWERPOINT A-16, POWERPOINT A-17

## F

**file(s)**. *See also* presentation(s)

closing, POWERPOINT A-16, POWERPOINT A-17

graphics, formats, POWERPOINT D-5

lost, recovering, POWERPOINT A-15

printing, POWERPOINT A-16, POWERPOINT A-17

saving, POWERPOINT A-12–13

**filenames**, POWERPOINT A-12

**Fill Effects dialog box**, POWERPOINT C-16

**font(s)**

saving with presentations, POWERPOINT A-12

selecting size, POWERPOINT C-12

**Font Color button**, POWERPOINT C-12

**footers**, slides, POWERPOINT B-10–11

**Format Table dialog box**, POWERPOINT D-12

**formatting**

charts, POWERPOINT D-10–11

text, POWERPOINT C-12–13

**Formatting toolbar**, POWERPOINT A-6, POWERPOINT A-7

## G

**Graph (program)**, POWERPOINT D-6, POWERPOINT D-7

**graphics formats**, POWERPOINT D-5

**grayscale**, viewing presentations, POWERPOINT A-17

**grouped objects**

animating parts, POWERPOINT D-18

grouping, POWERPOINT C-8, POWERPOINT C-9

**guides**, adding to slide, POWERPOINT C-8

## H

**header(s)**, slides, POWERPOINT B-10–11

**Header and Footer dialog box**, POWERPOINT B-10, POWERPOINT B-11

**Help system**, POWERPOINT A-14, POWERPOINT A-15

## I

**Ignore/Ignore All command**, POWERPOINT B-15

**importing text from Word**, POWERPOINT C-14–15

**Insert Chart button**, POWERPOINT D-6

**Insert Picture button**, POWERPOINT D-4

**installing PowerPoint**, POWERPOINT A-9

## J

**jumping to slides**, POWERPOINT D-14

## L

**lightbulb symbol**, meaning, POWERPOINT B-9

**line charts**, POWERPOINT D-7

**lost files**, recovering, POWERPOINT A-15

## M

**media clip placeholder**, POWERPOINT B-7

**menu(s)**, POWERPOINT A-6, POWERPOINT A-7. *See also specific menus*

**menu bar**, POWERPOINT A-6, POWERPOINT A-7

**Microsoft Office Web page**, clip art, POWERPOINT D-3

**moving**

objects, POWERPOINT D-2

text, POWERPOINT C-10

## ►N

**New Presentation task pane**, accessing, POWERPOINT A-8

**Normal view**, POWERPOINT A-6, POWERPOINT A-7, POWERPOINT A-10, POWERPOINT A-11

Outline tab, POWERPOINT B-8–9

Slide Design task pane, POWERPOINT B-12, POWERPOINT B-13

**notes**, POWERPOINT B-11

**Notes page view**, POWERPOINT A-11

**Notes pane**, POWERPOINT A-6, POWERPOINT A-7, POWERPOINT B-11

**Nudge button**, POWERPOINT D-2

## ►O

**objects**, POWERPOINT B-4, POWERPOINT C-5

aligning, POWERPOINT C-8, POWERPOINT C-9

changing order of animation, POWERPOINT D-18

drawing, POWERPOINT C-4, POWERPOINT C-5

drawn, editing, POWERPOINT C-6–7

grouped. *See* grouped objects

modifying, POWERPOINT C-4, POWERPOINT C-5

moving, POWERPOINT D-2

resizing, POWERPOINT C-4, POWERPOINT C-5

**opening**

existing presentations, POWERPOINT C-2–3

Save As dialog box, POWERPOINT C-2

**Order menu**, POWERPOINT C-7

**organization chart placeholder**, POWERPOINT B-7

**Outline tab**, POWERPOINT A-6, POWERPOINT A-7

entering text, POWERPOINT B-8–9

**Outlining toolbar**, POWERPOINT B-8

**overhead transparencies**, printing slides sized for, POWERPOINT A-16

## ►P

**panes**. *See also specific panes*

Normal view, POWERPOINT A-6, POWERPOINT A-7

**Paste button**, POWERPOINT C-10

**Paste command**, POWERPOINT C-10

**permissions**, setting, POWERPOINT C-3

**pictures**, inserting, POWERPOINT D-4, POWERPOINT D-5

**pie charts**, POWERPOINT D-7

**planning presentations**, POWERPOINT B-2–3

**PowerPoint**

exiting, POWERPOINT A-16, POWERPOINT A-17

features, POWERPOINT A-2, POWERPOINT A-3

installing, POWERPOINT A-9

starting, POWERPOINT A-4

**PowerPoint window**, POWERPOINT A-4, POWERPOINT A-5, POWERPOINT A-6–7

**presentation(s)**. *See also* file(s)

checklist for, POWERPOINT D-19

evaluating, POWERPOINT B-16–17

existing, opening, POWERPOINT C-2–3

planning, POWERPOINT B-2-3

reviewing, POWERPOINT C-11

saving, POWERPOINT A-12-13

saving fonts with presentations, POWERPOINT A-12

viewing in grayscale or black and white, POWERPOINT A-17

**presentation software**, POWERPOINT A-2–3

**Preset option button**, Fill Effects dialog box, POWERPOINT C-16

**Print button**, POWERPOINT A-16

**Print dialog box**, POWERPOINT A-16, POWERPOINT A-17

**Print Preview window**, POWERPOINT B-14, POWERPOINT B-15

**printing**

color, POWERPOINT A-16

files, POWERPOINT A-16, POWERPOINT A-17

notes, POWERPOINT B-11

**pyramid charts**, POWERPOINT D-7

## ►R

**radar charts**, POWERPOINT D-7

**recovering lost files**, POWERPOINT A-15

**rehearsing slide show timing**, POWERPOINT D-17

**replacing text and text attributes**, POWERPOINT C-13

**Research task pane**, POWERPOINT A-14, POWERPOINT A-15

**resizing objects**, POWERPOINT C-4, POWERPOINT C-5

**reviewing presentations**, POWERPOINT C-11

**rotate handle**, POWERPOINT C-6, POWERPOINT C-7

**rulers**, displaying, POWERPOINT C-6

## ►S

**Save As dialog box**, POWERPOINT A-12, POWERPOINT A-13

opening, POWERPOINT C-2

**saving**

annotations, POWERPOINT D-14

fonts with presentations, POWERPOINT A-12

presentations, POWERPOINT A-12–13

**scaling clip art**, POWERPOINT D-4, POWERPOINT D-5

**scatter charts**, POWERPOINT D-7

**Search Results task pane**, POWERPOINT A-14, POWERPOINT A-15

**Search the Web button**, Save As dialog box, POWERPOINT A-13

**Series in Columns command**, POWERPOINT D-9

**Series in Rows command**, POWERPOINT D-9

**Shadow Style menu**, POWERPOINT C-7

**shortcuts**, creating on desktop, POWERPOINT A-4

**slide(s)**

jumping to, POWERPOINT D-14

new, POWERPOINT B-6-7

notes, POWERPOINT B-11

from other presentations, inserting, POWERPOINT C-15

**Slide Design task pane**, POWERPOINT B-12, POWERPOINT B-13

opening, POWERPOINT B-12

**slide footers**, POWERPOINT B-10–11

**slide headers**, POWERPOINT B-10–11

**slide layouts**, POWERPOINT B-6, POWERPOINT B-7

**inserting clip art**, POWERPOINT D-2

**Slide pane**, POWERPOINT A-6, POWERPOINT A-7

**slide show(s)**

ending, POWERPOINT D-14

setting timings and transitions, POWERPOINT D-16–17

**Slide Show menu, buttons**, POWERPOINT D-14

**Slide Show view**, POWERPOINT A-11

annotations, POWERPOINT D-14

commands, POWERPOINT D-14–15

**Slide Sorter view**, POWERPOINT A-10, POWERPOINT A-11

**slide timings.** *See* timings

**slide transition(s)**, setting, POWERPOINT D-16–17

**Slide Transition task pane**, POWERPOINT D-16, POWERPOINT D-17

**Slides sized for list arrow**, Page Setup dialog box, POWERPOINT A-16

**Slides tab**, POWERPOINT A-6, POWERPOINT A-7

**speech recognition**, POWERPOINT B-5

**spell checking**, POWERPOINT B-14–15

**Spelling dialog box**, POWERPOINT B-14, POWERPOINT B-15

**Standard toolbar**, POWERPOINT A-6, POWERPOINT A-7

**starting PowerPoint**, POWERPOINT A-4

**status bar**, POWERPOINT A-6, POWERPOINT A-7

**stock charts**, POWERPOINT D-7

**Style menu**, POWERPOINT C-7

**subtitle text placeholders**, POWERPOINT B-4, POWERPOINT B-5

**Suggest command**, POWERPOINT B-15

**surface charts**, POWERPOINT D-7

## ►T

**table(s)**

cells. *See* table cells

changing cell height or width, POWERPOINT D-12

creating, POWERPOINT D-12–13

**table cells**

changing height or width, POWERPOINT D-12

diagonal line through, POWERPOINT D-12

**table placeholder**, POWERPOINT B-7

**task panes**, POWERPOINT A-6, POWERPOINT A-7. *See also specific task panes*

**templates**

multiple, POWERPOINT B-12

supplied with PowerPoint, POWERPOINT B-1, POWERPOINT B-12–13

from Web, POWERPOINT B-3

**text**

entering, POWERPOINT B-8–9

formatting, POWERPOINT C-12–13

importing from Word, POWERPOINT C-14–15

moving, POWERPOINT C-10, POWERPOINT C-11

replacing, POWERPOINT C-13

replacing attributes, POWERPOINT C-13

**text labels**, without text wrap, POWERPOINT C-10

**text objects**

adding, POWERPOINT C-10, POWERPOINT C-11

arranging, POWERPOINT C-10, POWERPOINT C-11

resizing, POWERPOINT C-4, POWERPOINT C-5

**text placeholders**, POWERPOINT B-4, POWERPOINT B-5

**thumbnails**, POWERPOINT A-6

**timings**

rehearsing, POWERPOINT D-16–17

setting, POWERPOINT D-16–17

**title bar**, POWERPOINT A-6, POWERPOINT A-7

**title placeholders**, POWERPOINT B-4, POWERPOINT B-5

**toolbars**, POWERPOINT A-6, POWERPOINT A-7. *See also specific toolbars*

**Tools button**, Save As dialog box, POWERPOINT A-13

**transitions**

slide shows, setting, POWERPOINT D-16–17

viewing, POWERPOINT D-14

 **U**

**Undo button list arrow**, POWERPOINT B-8

**Up One Level button**, Save As dialog box, POWERPOINT A-13

 **V**

**view(s)**, POWERPOINT A-6, POWERPOINT A-7. *See also specific views*

**view buttons**, POWERPOINT A-6, POWERPOINT A-7

**viewing presentations**, POWERPOINT A-10–11

in grayscale or black and white, POWERPOINT A-17

**viewing transitions**, POWERPOINT D-14

**Views button**, Save As dialog box, POWERPOINT A-13

**W**

**wizards**, POWERPOINT A-8, POWERPOINT A-9. *See also specific wizards*

**Word**, importing text from, POWERPOINT C-14–15

**X**

**XY charts**, POWERPOINT D-7